THE OTHER ORKNEY BOOK

THE OTHER ORKNEY BOOK

A Complete Pocket Guide

to

The Orkney Islands

BY GORDON THOMSON

WITH

REMARKS
ON THEIR PHYSICAL PECULIARITIES· HISTORY· PRODUCTIONS·
COMMERCE & CUSTOMS;

AND

GAZETTEERS
DESCRIBING PRINCIPAL ARCHAEOLOGICAL SITES· HISTORIC
MONUMENTS· TOWNS· ISLANDS· AMENITIES
&C. , &C.;

ALSO A

GLOSSARY OF PLACE-NAMES
WITH THEIR MEANINGS.

Illustrated by Ethel Walker, D.A.

NORTHABOUT PUBLISHING

EDINBURGH

© Gordon Thomson 1980

First published 1980

ISBN 0 907200 00 1

Published by Northabout Publishing, 57 Warrender Park Road, Edinburgh
Printed in Great Britain by Waterside Printers, Blanefield, Stirlingshire
Typesetting by Famedram Publishers Limited, Gartocharn, Dunbartonshire

CONTENTS

ACKNOWLEDGMENTS

The author would like to thank the following for their
invaluable assistance and co-operation in the production of
this book:
**George Mackay Brown, Liz Tait, Tam & Gunnie
MacPhail, Irene Sinclair, Sue MacDougall, Alistair
Allport** and many others too numerous to mention.
Also—**Orkney Islands Council, Orkney Tourist
Organisation, Orkney Libraries, Department of the
Environment** and **National Museum of Antiquities of
Scotland.**

The final content of this book and any views expressed within
it, however, may be attributed to the author alone.

KEY TO ORKNEY MAPS

Brochs

16. Gurness *(Mainland)*
28. Midhowe *(Rousay)*

Cairns - chambered

9. Cuween *(Mainland)*
18. Holm of Papa Westray
26. Maeshowe *(Mainland)*
35. Quoyness *(Sanday)*
50. Wideford Hill *(Mainland)*

Cairns - stalled

4. Blackhammer *(Rousay)*
25. Knowe of Yarso *(Rousay)*
29. Midhowe *(Rousay)*
33. Onston *(Mainland)*
46. Taversoe Tuick *(Rousay)*

Cairns - horned

17. Head of Work *(Mainland)*
22. Knowe of Lairso *(Rousay)*

Castles & Palaces

3. Bishop's Palace *(Kirkwall)*
8. Cubbie Roo's Castle *(Wyre)*
11. Earl's Palace *(Birsay)*
12. Earl's Palace (Kirkwall)
30. Noltland Castle *(Westray)*

Chapels & Churches

5. Brough of Birsay *(Mainland)*
13. Eynhallow
19. Italian Chapel *(Lamb Holm)*
34. Orphir Round Church *(Mainland)*
38. St. Magnus Cathedral *(Kirkwall)*
39. St. Magnus Church *(Egilsay)*
40. St. Tredwell's Chapel *(Papa Westray)*
41. Skaill *(Mainland)*
49. Westray Churches *(Westray)*
52. Wyre Chapel *(Wyre)*

Cists

23. Knowe of Smirrus *(Mainland)*

24. Knowes of Trotty *(Mainland)*

Earth-houses

15. Grain *(Mainland)*
36. Rennibister *(Mainland)*

Menhirs

37. Ring of Brogar *(Mainland)*
43. Stones of Stenness *(Mainland)*

Mills

1. Barony Mill *(Mainland)*
7. Click Mill *(Mainland)*
47. Tormiston Mill *(Mainland)*

Museums

14. Graemshall *(Mainland)*
16. Gurness Broch *(Mainland)*
42. Skara Brae *(Mainland)*
44. Stromness *(Mainland)*
45. Tankerness House *(Kirkwall)*

Old Dwellings

2. Bimbister *(Mainland)*
27. Midhouse *(Mainland)*
51. Winksetter *(Mainland)*

Settlements

5. Brough of Birsay *(Mainland)*
21. Knap of Howar *(Papa Westray)*
34. Orphir - Earl's Bu *(Mainland)*
35. Skaill *(Mainland)*
42. Skara Brae *(Mainland)*
48. Westness *(Rousay)*

Miscellaneous

6. Churchill Barriers
10. Dwarfie Stone *(Hoy)*
20. Kirkwall *(Mainland)*
31. North Gaulton Castle *(Mainland)*
32. Old Man of Hoy
44. Stromness *(Mainland)*

Regular service airfield   Important seabird cliff   Licensed premises (L)

Golf course   Caravan site   Camping site ▲

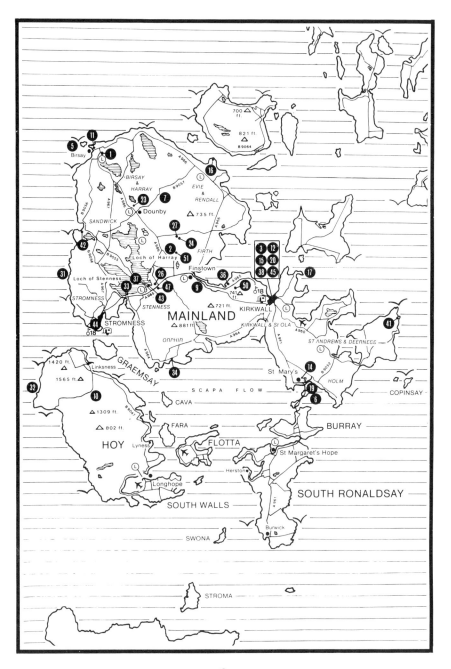

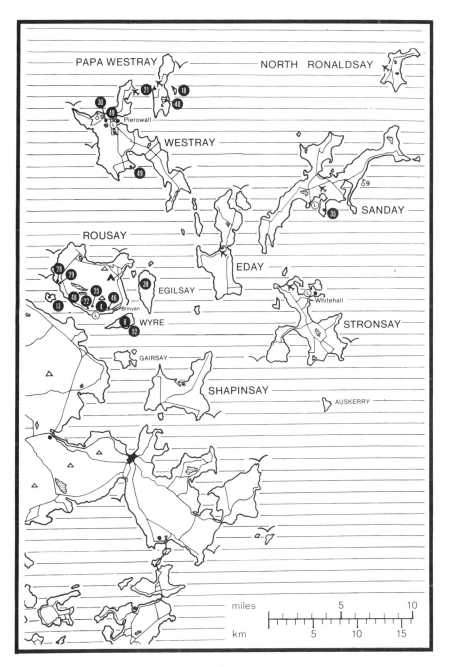

STROMNESS

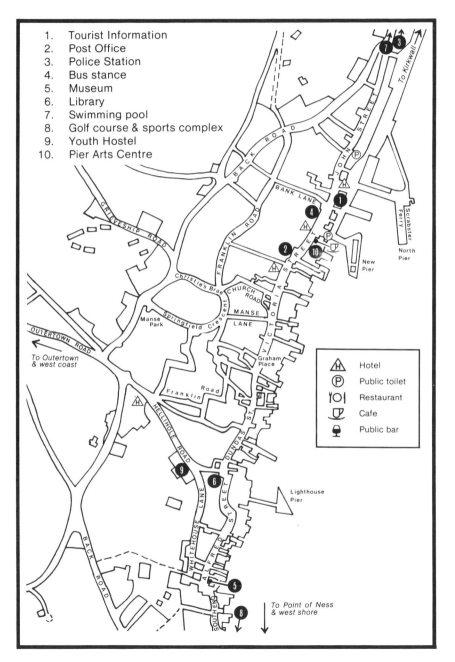

1. Tourist Information
2. Post Office
3. Police Station
4. Bus stance
5. Museum
6. Library
7. Swimming pool
8. Golf course & sports complex
9. Youth Hostel
10. Pier Arts Centre

Hotel
Public toilet
Restaurant
Cafe
Public bar

To Kirkwall

Scrabster Ferry

North Pier

New Pier

To Outertown & west coast

Lighthouse Pier

To Point of Ness & west shore

NORTHERN ISLES

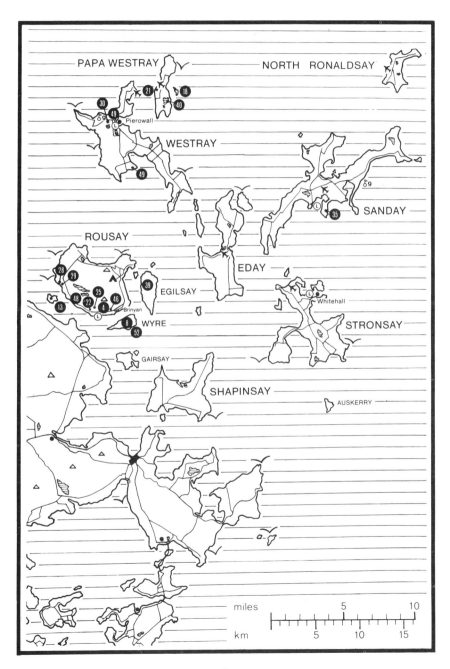

PAPA WESTRAY

NORTH RONALDSAY

WESTRAY

Pierowall

SANDAY

ROUSAY

EDAY

EGILSAY

Brinyan

WYRE

Whitehall

STRONSAY

GAIRSAY

SHAPINSAY

AUSKERRY

miles   5   10

km   5   10   15

STROMNESS

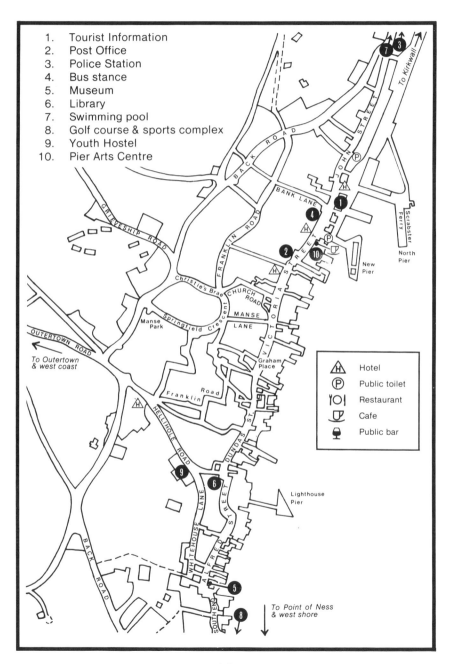

1. Tourist Information
2. Post Office
3. Police Station
4. Bus stance
5. Museum
6. Library
7. Swimming pool
8. Golf course & sports complex
9. Youth Hostel
10. Pier Arts Centre

Hotel
Public toilet
Restaurant
Cafe
Public bar

KIRKWALL

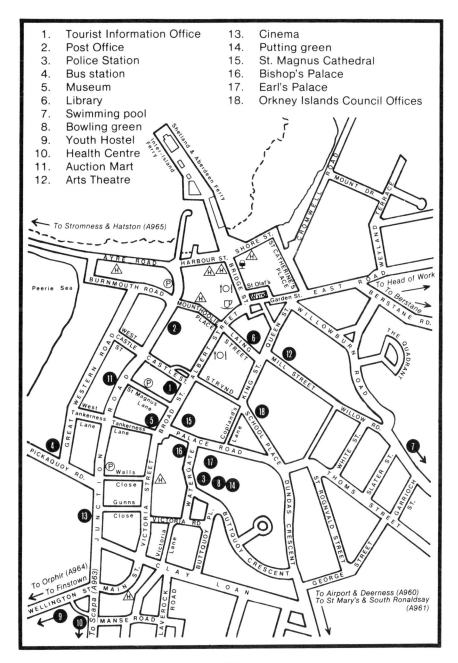

1. Tourist Information Office
2. Post Office
3. Police Station
4. Bus station
5. Museum
6. Library
7. Swimming pool
8. Bowling green
9. Youth Hostel
10. Health Centre
11. Auction Mart
12. Arts Theatre

13. Cinema
14. Putting green
15. St. Magnus Cathedral
16. Bishop's Palace
17. Earl's Palace
18. Orkney Islands Council Offices

Shetland & Aberdeen Ferry

Inter-Island Ferry

To Stromness & Hatston (A965)

Peerie Sea

AYRE ROAD

HARBOUR ST.

SHORE ST.

ST CATHERINE'S PLACE

CROMWELL ROAD

MOUNT DR.

WEYLAND TERRACE

BURNMOUTH ROAD

BRIDGE ST.

St Olaf's

EAST ROAD

To Head of Work
To Berstane

BERSTANE RD.

MOUNTHOOLIE PLACE

Garden St.

Wynd

WILLOWBURN ROAD

THE QUADRANT

WEST CASTLE ST.

LAING STREET

QUEEN ST.

MILL STREET

GREAT WESTERN ROAD

CASTLE ST.

ST. ALBERT ST.

STRYND

KING ST.

WILLOW RD.

West Tankerness Lane

Tankerness Lane

St Magnus Lane

BROAD ST.

Copland's Lane

SCHOOL PLACE

WHITE ST.

THOMS STREET

SLATER ST.

GARRIOCH ST.

PICKAQUOY RD.

JUNCTION ROAD

PALACE ROAD

DUNDAS CRESCENT

ST ROGNVALD STREET

GEORGE STREET

Walls

Close

Gunns

Close

VICTORIA STREET

WATERGATE

BUTTQUOY PL.

VICTORIA RD.

Victoria Lane

BUTTQUOY CRESCENT

To Orphir (A964)
To Finstown

WELLINGTON ST.

MAIN ST.

CLAY LOAN

LAVEROCK ROAD

GEORGE STREET

To Airport & Deerness (A960)
To St Mary's & South Ronaldsay (A961)

To Scapa (A963)

MANSE ROAD

11

Orkney - a Brief Outline

I N THIS MATERIALISTIC AGE it is all too easy to forget that a nation's
most valuable resource is neither its mineral deposits nor its
technological superiority, but that which makes everything else
possible—its people. In this respect the British Isles are richly endowed,
with an abundant variety of indigenous cultures and ethnic denomi-
nations. Although dividing lines inevitably become blurred and differences less marked with the passage of time (who today can recognise
a Pict?), nevertheless differences there are: and nowhere do they remain
so apparent as in our offshore islands . . .

A mere six sea-swept miles separate the Orkney Islands and
mainland Scotland; yet—as anyone who has ever ventured across that
tract of contentious tides and currents will tell you—milestones are not
always the best test of distance. Despite its proximity and long-standing
allegiance to 'the adjacent island of Great Britain', this former outpost
of Norse dominion remains firmly rooted in its own unique traditions
and ways—a land of resolutely independent character and strange
elemental beauty.

Of the hundred or so isles, rocks and skerries of which it is composed,
some sixty-seven can safely be called 'Islands', around twenty of these
being inhabited. They lie at a latitude only 50 m. south of Greenland,
extend for 53 m. in one direction and 30 m. in the other, boast coastlines
which total an astonishing 570 m. and, altogether, occupy 376 sq.m.

The Orkney Islands can be broken down into three basic groups—the
Northern Isles, the Southern Isles and Mainland. This last island
(formerly and incorrectly frequently referred to as *Pomona*) constitutes
more than half of Orkney's land-mass and accommodates over two-

13

thirds of its entire population.

Orkney has been inhabited by man for more than five millennia—longer than many areas of Britain. By 1861 its population had grown to 32,000. Today, however, this figure has been virtually halved, with a population level bordering on 18,000. The citizens of Kirkwall and Stromness—Orkney's two towns—number respectively 4,800 and 1,700. There are indications that Orkney's overall population is beginning to stabilise, although depopulation in the outer islands is still a problem.

Orcadians are very mobile people, with a car to person ratio of 1:3—one of the highest in Britain. With a scattered populace living in outlying rural areas, however, the need for mobility is great: the wherewithal to acquire it is rarely lacking either, as average savings figures show—Orkney is a prosperous island community.

To continue in statistical vein, Orkney can boast one site of historical interest to every sixteen people; three to every square mile; or, in blunt terms, over 1,000—probably the greatest density in Britain. This wealth of palpable antiquity, amongst other things, attracts nearly 70,000 visitors (local idiom—*ferryloupers*) to these islands every summer, and, in doing so, contributes considerably to the Orcadian economy. Orkney's principle source of wealth, however, is agriculture—especially beef production, followed in descending order of economic return by distilling, tourism, knitwear production, fishing and boatbuilding. (See *The Land* and *Industry*.)

The Orkney Islands may lack trees, fall down on mountains, and display little of that brooding, Wagnerian melodrama so typical of Highland landscape; but they possess a beauty and atmosphere of their own which would be invidious to draw comparisons with. The pervading impression is one of uninhibited space: rolling countryside, low, undulating hills, and a sweeping confluence of sea, sky and land—a land checkered with evenly distributed farms, pastures and cultivated fields. Although Orkney has its wild places—notably Hoy—few areas are outwith sight of sea or habitation. Villages and tightly gathered communities are relatively few and far between, however: such as there are, in most instances, evolved around the sea, with its associated

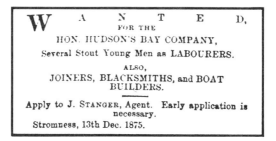

WANTED,
FOR THE
HON. HUDSON'S BAY COMPANY,
Several Stout Young Men as LABOURERS.
ALSO,
JOINERS, BLACKSMITHS, and BOAT BUILDERS.

Apply to J. STANGER, Agent. Early application is necessary.
Stromness, 13th Dec. 1875.

trading and fishing concerns, rather than the land. This is equally true of Kirkwall and Stromness.

Despite the passage of time, changing fortunes (particularly during the rule and depredations of the Stewart Earldom) and the reorganisation of land in the 18th and 19th centuries, some properties have remained within the ambit of the same families for hundreds of years. The Hall of Rendall is owned by the Halcros—a family of Norse origin which is reputed to be descended from a Norse king, and related by marriage to the Scottish Royal House—and they have held title to their estate for nearly a millennium. The Linklater family of Upper Housgarth can made a similar claim; and it is said that twenty-four families in the parish of Birsay have farmed the same land for more than 400 years.

The parishes of Mainland may have been delineated in Norse times, but it is equally possible that their boundaries had already been decided and laid down before then, by the Picts. Certainly, they were pre-Christian in origin, and administrative in purpose. The origin of the word 'Orkney' itself remains open to debate; but it could well have derived from the conjunction of two words—the Celtic word *orc*, signifying a wild boar, and the Norse suffix *ey*, or island, sometimes written *a* or *ay*. Thus: 'Islands of the People of the Wild Boar'.

Although many factors combined to shape Orkney into the end product we see today, its fertile and easily-worked soil must rank high amongst these. It was appreciated and used to advantage both by its first neolithic settlers—armed only with primitive implements—and by land-hungry Norsemen more than 4,000 years later. Past events are related elsewhere, but the Norse influence cannot be over-stressed, and is still much in evidence throughout Orkney: in the curious gable-ended houses of Kirkwall (which lend the town a piquant, foreign flavour); in the niceties of land-tenure; in the absence of private fishing rights (almost); in the style of local boat-building; and—most of all—in the preponderance of Norse place-names and surnames.

Norse gave way to English as the official language in the 15th century, after Orkney was pledged to Scotland, but for long after that it was to linger on in the form of the Orkney Norn, a local dialect derivative of old Norse. Some words are still in common use (e.g. *peedie*—small), but as a working language it has died out. Some of the older members of the community, however, especially on the more remote islands, may still present the stranger with comprehension problems.

Separated from each other by the storm-tossed waters of the Pentland Firth, the influence of Scotland (and Scottish ways) on Orkney was much diluted, and such innovations as were effected by Scottish rule did not dispose Orcadians kindly towards their new landlords. In any case, such links as were forged were, in most instances, with the Scottish Lowlands, and at no stage did Orkney become seriously involved with the Celt or Gael, perhaps unfortunately. However, by the same token, the political and religious conflicts which rampaged and flared throughout Scotland in the 17th and 18th centuries caused comparatively few ripples in Orkney. Even in these enlightened times the typical Orcadian is a model of dispassionate free-thinking.

Orkney's meteorological conduct can be less equable, however. Gales and strong winds can occur at any time of year: In 1969 one of the strongest gusts ever recorded (136mph) blew a chicken-coop one mile out to sea, and the gales of January 1952 and '53 respectively caused £0.5m. damage to agriculture, and wrecked Kirkwall's sea-front. So much for the bad news!: extremes of hot or cold are unusual, thanks to the tempering effects of sea and Gulf Stream, and Orkney rarely experiences thunderstorms or heavy snow. Although the winter can be dark and dismal, the long hours of daylight in summer months more than compensate—on Midsummer's Day the sun is above the horizon for 18¼ hours and one can indulge in golf or photography at midnight. Sunsets of remarkable beauty are frequent, especially during the months May—July. On average Orkney's driest months are April—June, and its wettest month, December, although this can vary. Orkney's climate is fresh and invigorating, and its landscape leaves the wind free to indulge its moods (whether breeze or blast) unimpeded. For this reason trees do not flourish here to any great extent, and rather than trees sheltering houses, the reverse is true—Orkney's tallest trees are urban dwellers.

The elements may behave with scant inhibition now and again, but full atonement is invariably made: such are the matchless days when a bright blue mantle unfolds and encompasses all as far as the eye can see; days when the sun-burnished expanses of Orkney dwell in a serenity and timelessness as deep as the skies are wide—on such occasions the passage of centuries is an affair which seems to hang as lightly as the wheeling gulls above.

Origins & Evolution

ORKNEY WAS HONED to its present smooth contours by the action of retreating Scandinavian ice sheets which finally vanished some 10,000 years ago. The Climate warmed up, and by 7500 B·C· a warm, boreal period was established. During this continental era trees such as rowan, birch, hazel and elder flourished in Orkney and conditions were very different from today's. The sea-level was lower too, as evinced by the discovery of preserved remains of trees in the clay of submerged beaches. Circa 5500 B·C· the climate deteriorated, becoming wetter and more windy, although still mild by today's standards. This was the Atlantic period, towards the end of which Orkney's first settlers arrived, and during which most of Orkney's trees decayed and vanished, to become in time the basis of the Islands' peat beds. By 2500 B·C· the climate was on the turn again, and a warm, sub-boreal period developed. About 700 B·C·, however, the climate underwent another reverse, and the cooler, wetter, sub-Atlantic period which persists today set in.

The earliest accepted presence of man in Scotland occurs during the mesolithic or Middle Stone Age, which—in Scotland at least—began around 6000 B·C· These first inhabitants were itinerant hunters and *food-gatherers*. Some few of the small worked flints or *microliths* which date from this period have been found in Orkney, and suggest a small-scale human occupation even then; however, settlement had not yet begun.

THE FIRST SETTLERS

The neolithic or Late Stone Age was characterised by revolutionary cultural developments, and marked the beginnings of civilization as we know it. The people who appear during this period were settlers and *food-producers*. Writing of this era, Professor J.H. Plumb says, '...it diversified human life and thought and provided conditions infinitely more stimulating to man's intellectual capacities than his earlier modes of living.'

Orkney's neolithic immigrants sailed their frail boats over the Pentland Firth for the first time during the 4th millennium B·C·, leaving behind them a Scotland which consisted largely of impenetrable marshland and forest: Orkney, with its freedom from predators, fertile soil and remoteness, offered these peaceful herdsmen and farmers a welcome security. At that time Orkney was rich in red deer and wildfowl; fish and shellfish were plentiful; Stone Age Man brought sheep, cattle and seed-corn with him; for fuel he had peat, driftwood and the remains of the Boreal forests at his disposal; the climate was becoming kinder—all things considered, life must have been reasonably tolerable.

During the next 1,500 years or so these pastoral people were to create and bequeath to Orkney a wealth of archaeological interest which has few parallels elsewhere in Britain, although their funerary customs have antecedents which can be visibly traced down the coasts of both Britain and Ireland--and on through Brittany, Spain and Portugal to the Eastern Mediterranean. It is probable that these were the anterior homes of Orkney's neolithic inhabitants. What spurred them to venture so far north is uncertain, but it may have been sheer pressure of numbers: the density of monuments in Orkney suggests that the size of its neolithic population may have approached present-day levels.

NEOLITHIC MONUMENTS

Late Stone Age Man was a prolific and skilled mason, and the channel into which much of his energy was diverted and found expression was the creation of a multitude of ingenious tombs. Such are Orkney's cairns, and these fall into two basic groups, albeit with a great measure of individual variety, and, in some instances, possessing features of both. The 'chambered' cairn, of which **Maeshowe** is the finest example, generally takes the form of a central, stone-lined chamber with small, radiating mural cells, approached by a relatively long and narrow passageway leading into the heart of the mound. The style was probably introduced by a fresh wave of settlers during the early 3rd millennium B·C· Similar tombs may be found in Ireland. The other main type, the Orkney-Cromarty-Hebridean or 'stalled' cairn, pre-dates the

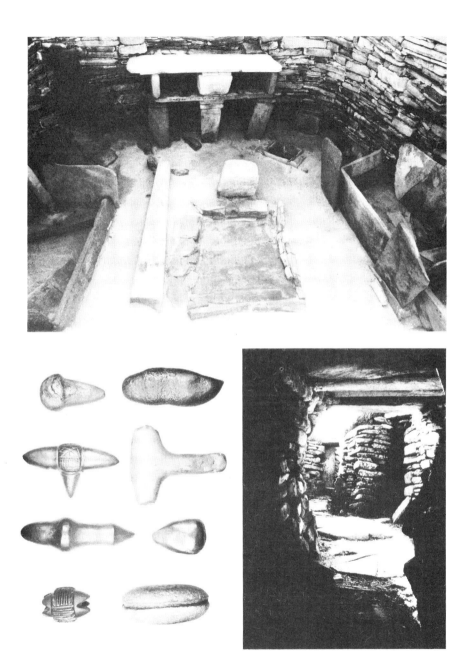

TOP Skara Brae hut interior. BOTTOM LEFT Stone artifacts excavated at Skara Brae: *Department of the Environment.* BOTTOM RIGHT A flagstone covered passageway at Skara Brae.

19

TOP The massive, 18½ft. high Watch Stone at Bridge of Brodgar, Stenness.
BOTTOM The Ring of Brogar (detail).

Maeshowe variety and was in vogue from the mid-4th to mid-3rd millennia B·C· It usually consists of an elongated, narrow chamber, divided into smaller compartments or 'stalls' by upright stone slabs along each of the longer sides—with a central passageway left clear, and entered via a relatively short, stone-lined tunnel. The best examples of this type are found on Rousay. Reference should also be made to that sub-species of stalled cairn know as 'horned' cairns—so-called because of the bipartite earthwork projecting from either end of the cairn, forming enclosures. Only three examples have been discovered in Orkney, being more common in Caithness. One was recorded last century on Burray, but no trace of it can be found today. The others are at **Head of Work** near Kirkwall, and on Rousay (**Knowe of Lairso**).

The cairns are regarded as family or communal tombs which were continuously used over a long period. Inhumation was customary, although cremation was sometimes practiced. Many relics have been discovered within them, including flint and stone implements, and pottery—the collection of pottery which was unearthed at **Onston Cairn** being of special importance. The earth and turf covering of some cairns, when removed, has revealed great architectural, and frequently decorative detail; which begs the question—were they thus covered by man, or was it the work of time and the elements? Many of their Mediterranean counterparts are located below ground-level: perhaps some dim race-memory of this prescribed burial beneath the soil.

The architecture of death is not the only tangible reminder of Stone Age Man to survive in Orkney, however: **Skara Brae** and the **Knap of Howar** (respectively, one of the finest neolithic villages, and probably the oldest stone house still standing in North-West Europe) both give us tantalising glimpses of his domestic life. The mysterious stone circles of **Brogar** and **Stenness** stand testimony to his imagination, and, perhaps, his state of awareness—although the exact purpose of these ambitious megaliths remains to be deciphered, it has been argued that their arrangement involved a sophisticated knowledge of mathematics and astronomy.

The cairn-builders left hundreds of conspicuous reminders of their epoch, but the period which follows theirs was to be considerably less prolific . . . .

BRONZE AGE

The earliest record of copper-smelting is found in Turkey around 6000 B·C·, but knowledge of this art did not arrive in Britain until another 4,000 years had passed. The people who introduced it into these sceptred Isles are referred to as *Beaker folk*, after the characteristic shape of their pottery. Small numbers of them reached Orkney, and with them came knowledge of bronze. But the term 'Bronze Age' is a misnomer when applied to Orkney: very little evidence of bronze-working has been found, and it is apparent that the conventional use of stone implements continued well into Orkney's so-called Bronze Age. This epoch remains largely a misty landscape of half-answered questions and continuing speculation; but that a flowering of ideas occurred, and that radical cultural changes took place is certain.

Burial rites, for instance, increasingly involved single interment in small slab-lined cists, sometimes covered over by a low earthen barrow or stone cairn—such are the tumuli in the vicinity of Brogar. However, the practice of inhumation eventually died out, and gave way to cremation.

Most of the single, isolated standing stones are believed to date from the Bronze Age; as are 'burnt mounds'—the remains of primitive cooking sites. Such earth-houses as **Grain** *may* date from the end of this era, but the lack of dateable artifacts precludes verification, and souterrains remain one of archaeology's enigmas. Indeed, this phenomenon is the principal cause of the uncertainty which shrouds this period in Orkney's history—and of that which was to follow.

IRON AGE

The term 'Iron Age', when applied to Orkney, is again descriptive of a period which brought knowledge of a new skill, rather than one which saw its widespread application: the Early Iron Age heralded a subtle transition from virtual non-use of one metal to non-use of another. However, this period witnessed an influx of new settlers during the 6th and 5th centuries B·C·, with a further wave during the 3rd century B·C·

Life may have continued in a fairly peaceful manner for some time, but this was not to last: Throughout Britain the 1st century B·C·—1st century A·D· was characterised by insurgence, power struggles, rivalries, raiding expeditions and invasion. Orkney was in a strong position, however, and it is said that in A·D· 43 Orcadian chiefs made treaty with the Romans. According to Tacitus, in A·D· 78 Julius Agricola led an expedition to the Northern Isles.

The broch emerged around this time to meet its defensive needs. Its curious structure appears to have developed in the Hebrides, from whence it rapidly spread to Orkney, and thence to Caithness and Shetland. The broch is virtually confined to the north of Scotland, there being 102, out of a total of 500 in Scotland, located in Orkney. The brochs are so similar in design and construction that one could be forgiven for suspecting the same architect or architect's plan was responsible for all of them. The best preserved example extant is the *Broch of Mousa* in Shetland. The general configuration of these

Reconstruction view of broch and wheel-house post settlement.
(Reproduced by courtesy of the 'Illustrated London News')

structures is a circular, bell-shaped tower, varying in diameter from 40-80 ft. at the base, where the wall is usually solid and 10-15 ft. thick. Narrow, concentric galleries connected by flights of steps run within the wall to the top of the broch—originally up to 50 ft. high. These passages functioned as a form of inbuilt scaffolding, facilitating the transportation of stone upwards, while simultaneously making great saving in the total amount used without weakening the structure. From the exterior the broch was virtually impregnable; the only chink in its stony armour was a small entrance tunnel which would have been firmly sealed against unwelcome visitors. The two best-known and excavated examples in Orkney are those of **Gurness** and **Midhowe**. The brochs may well have been a development of such stone-built forts as *Clickhimin* in Shetland, sharing, as they do, such features as intramural galleries and timber ranges around the inner wall. On the basis that there were 102 brochs in Orkney and that each—it is estimated—could probably accommodate between 50-100 people, the population of Orkney may well have totalled some 5,000-10,000 during the 1st century A·D·.

THE PICTS

That recondite race known as the *Picts*—who, it is thought, were of Scandinavian origin, and about whom so much has been written, said and conjectured—emerged as silently as they disappeared. Brochs were frequently referred to as 'Picts' Castles', but they had fallen into partial decay by the period of Pictish ascendency. The first recorded reference to the Picts' existence dates from A·D· 297, when the Romans so denoted the inhabitants of northern Scotland who were neither *Scots* nor *Britons*. The name probably derived from the Latin term *picti*, or painted—i.e. 'The Painted Ones'.

Pictish political dominance was well established by the end of the 6th century A·D·, and their kingdom extended through East and Lowland Scotland. Although the Romans took a dim view of their level of culture, they possessed a remarkable skill in metal-working: Many fine and beautiful examples of their bronze brooches, rings, pins, massive armulets and harness-mountings—some enamelled—have been found in Scotland, along with silver chains, glass beads, and tools and ornaments in stone, bone and wood—often intricately carved. Examples of Pictish art identified in Orkney include a carved symbol-stone from **Brough of Birsay** (around 250 such monuments have been discovered throughout N & E Scotland, dating from A·D· 600-900: their exact purpose remains obscure, although tombstones, territorial boundary markers and commemorative monuments to important marriages have all been proposed) and a bone knife-handle from **Gurness Broch** bearing inscribed *ogam* script—an alphabet unfortunately unintelligible and probably based on a language now lost to us (one of two tongues believed used by the Picts—the other being a Celtic variant). During the Picts' era the brochs, although semi-dilapidated, continued to be inhabited, and many of the structures tacked onto and within them date from this period.

CELTIC MISSIONS

When the Norse arrived in Orkney they found two classes of people— the *Peti* and the *Papae.* The former were the Picts; the latter were the clergy of the early Celtic missions. Little trace of these dedicated men of peace remains. Their existence is dimly remembered in some place-names: *Papa Westray, Papa Stronsay,* etc. Only a handful of sites can be attributed to them with any certainty, and all are of an isolated character. Amongst these rank the **Brough of Birsay,** the *Brough of Deerness* (**Skaill**), and **Eynhallow** (although this last is still in dispute). Apart from these 7th-century missions, the Celt did not infiltrate Orkney significantly—the early Celtic Church had strong affiliations with the Scots, who were bitter rivals of the Picts to the extent of open warfare. The Columban hermit, Cormac, travelled to Orkney in order to baptise its inhabitants only after he had been given assurance of safe-conduct by the Pictish king, Bruide MacMaelchon (*Bridei*) in 584— during St Columba's visit to Bruide's hill-fort near Inverness, where his famous battle-of-words with the druidic priests took place. Although this safe-conduct saved Cormac's life on at least two occasions, it is worth relating that his evangelical mission did not rely entirely on the offices of faith and good-will for a successful outcome—a warlike expedition, led by Ædan, King of the Dalriad Scots, descended on Orkney prior to Cormac's arrival, and doubtless persuaded many Picts of the merits of Christianity. Thereafter the Islands remained under the dominion of the Dalriads for almost 100 years, until 682, when the North Picts reconquered them.

NORSEMEN

The Orcadian Picts were overwhelmed by the Norse in the late 8th and early 9th centuries. Nowhere else in Britain did they colonise so successfully as the Northern Isles. Much of Ireland fell to their might, but they were later to be ousted by the Irish, and little trace of their rule remains there today. In Orkney their influence was to last.

Reconstruction view of a typical Later Norse settlement.
(Reproduced by courtesy of the 'Illustrated London News')

The Norse were by no means entirely a race of ruthless predators: previous to the Viking onslaught around A·D· 800 settlers had already started to arrive, and by 850 colonisation was well under way. The sovereignty of the Norse Crown was established in Orkney by King Harald Haarfager in 872, when he made a punitive expedition against rival and ousted Norse chieftains who had continued to openly defy him. Christianity lingered on in Orkney in a subdued role, and, we must assume, was absorbed into the crowded polytheistic cosmology of the incoming Norse to an extent: but Orkney's new overlords remained overtly pagan in their beliefs and ways. Even when Christianity was officially adopted in 995 by King Olaf of Norway (later Saint Olaf), his subjects frequently interpreted it in a less than conventional manner!

By the 10th century the power of the Norse earls of Orkney was firmly rooted. Conflict sometimes arose between these earls and their king in Norway: Earl Thorfinn Sigurdsson, the mightiest of all, only staved off Norwegian retribution with a mixture of cunning, statesmanship and luck. This legendary figure eventually ruled Orkney, Shetland, the Hebrides, part of Scotland and a realm in Ireland from the small tidal island, **Brough of Birsay**, where he built a small cathedral church and palace. He made pilgrimage to Rome—with King Macbeth, to whom he was related—to seek absolution for his bloody past, and, respected and ruling still, died peacefully in 1064, aged 75. (His widow, Ingibiörg, later married Malcolm Canmore, King of Scotland.)

The St Magnus of cathedral fame was Thorfinn's grandson, Magnus Erlendsson: as Earl Magnus he ruled Orkney jointly with his cousin and fellow-earl, Haakon Paulsson. By nature a man of peace, Magnus agreed to meet Haakon in an attempt to settle the differences which had arisen between them—and riven Orkney into warring factions.

Magnus arrived at the trysting-place, the small island of Egilsay, on the appointed day—April 16th, 1115—with two ships and a small force of unarmed men, as agreed on previously. (It is said that, despite a calm sea, a freak wave almost swamped Magnus's ship during the voyage: his men feared this to be an ill omen, and entreated him to turn back; to no avail—Magnus would not be moved.) When Haakon eventually appeared it was with a total of eight ships and a large body of armed men ... there was to be no discussion. Magnus bowed gracefully to his fate, and, after spending the night in prayer, went quietly to his martyrdom the following day at the hands of Haakon's henchmen. (Haakon was afterwards seized with remorse at this deed; he made pilgimage to Jerusalem in penance [1116-18] and eventually died as a beloved ruler in 1222 or 3.) His body was interred in Christ Church, Birsay; and less than 200 years later—following many reputed miracles—Magnus was canonised. Today his relics (complete with gaping axe wound in the skull) rest in the cathedral in Kirkwall.

This imposing building was begun in 1137 by Magnus's nephew, Earl Rognvald, who more than any man represented the zenith of Norse culture in Orkney—he was a poet, could pluck a harp as well as he could wield an axe, and his court in Kirkwall attracted many men of intellect. (The source of much of our knowledge of Norse Orkney is that vivid and admirable book, the *Orkneyinga Saga*, written around 1220.)

During the 13th century Norwegian authority over Orkney dwindled rapidly. When King Haakon passed through in 1230, en route to the

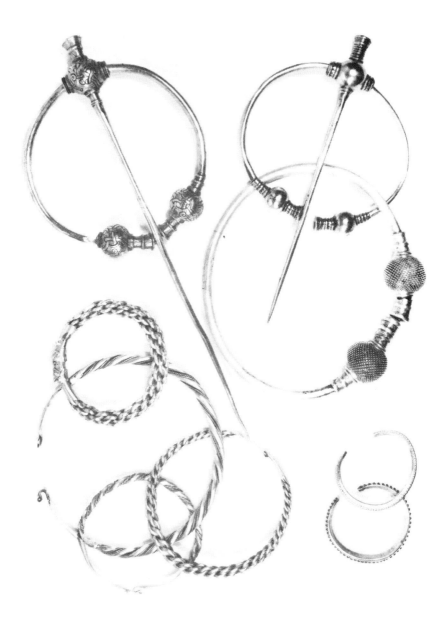

Silver jewellery from the Viking treasure-hoard which was excavated at Skaill, Mainland: *National Museum of Antiquities of Scotland.*

TOP LEFT The nave, St. Magnus Cathedral, Kirkwall. TOP RIGHT The Earl's Palace, Kirkwall. BOTTOM Aerial view of Gurness Broch: *Gunnie Moberg.*

Hebrides, Arran, and the Isle of Man, and intent on re-asserting Norse sovereignty and quashing Scottish claims and incursions, he recruited half his forces in Orkney. However, when his son, King Haakon IV, repeated the exercise in 1263 he failed to recruit any men; and—after a protracted and abortive campaign—he returned to Kirkwall a broken man, and soon succumbed to an illness of which he died ten days before Christmas in the **Bishop's Palace.** (Shortly after this the disputed provinces were finally ceded to Scotland.)

TRANSFER OF POWER

The last direct Norse earl of Orkney, Earl John Haraldsson, died in 1231, murdered in a cellar in Thurso. Following this the earldom passed to the Earls of Angus—a lineage with distinct Scottish ties. When the last Angus earl of Orkney, Magnus the Fifth, died around 1321, the earldom passed through the female line to the Earl of Strathearn, a Scot, and in 1379 to his grandson—the most powerful and popular of the Scottish earls of Orkney, Earl Henry Sinclair the First. During his rule Orkney moved even farther from the Norwegian sphere of influence, and old allegiances were called into question with increasing frequency. By the second quarter of the 14th century immigration from Scotland and use of the Scots tongue were already under way in Orkney. Earl Henry Sinclair went one step further and built a castle in Kirkwall in defiance of the Norwegian Crown (in addition, he is reputed to have sailed to America).

By 1468, when Orkney was mortgaged to Scotland, many Scots had settled in the Islands: the Scottish connection was firmly established, and the transfer of effective power seemed a logical, almost inevitable conclusion. At this juncture Norway, Sweden and Denmark were united under one throne—that of King Christian the First, a Dane (and one not greatly interested in Norwegian colonial affairs; Orkney being one of many problems he inherited along with the Norse Crown). Scotland and Denmark shared strong commercial and military interests; nonetheless, *entente* was endangered by King Christian's demands for back-payment of the annual tributes which Scotland had previously undertaken—and long neglected—to pay upon acquiring the Western Isles from Norway. Eventually, as a means of healing the breach which had arisen, it was proposed that King Christian's daughter, Margaret, should marry King James III of Scotland. A dowry of 60,000 florins was agreed on; Orkney being pledged for 50,000 florins, the remainder to be paid in cash. Within a year only 2,000 florins were forthcoming, and Shetland was pledged for the 8,000 florin balance—an interesting comparison. The pledges were never redeemed (it is probable that by tacit agreement they were never intended to be); and two years later both the earldom of Orkney and the Lordship of Shetland were annexed by the Scottish Crown. During the following centuries, however, Orcadians were to be given ample cause to regret this bargain.

King James's first act upon acquiring Orkney was in 1471 to compel Earl William Sinclair to exchange his earldom for another in Fife and appoint himself in his place. He did not rule directly, setting up tacksmen to govern by proxy instead.

A rebellion broke out in 1528 against the misrule of the then incumbent tacksman, led by James Sinclair, governor of Kirkwall Castle and a descendant of the earlier Sinclair earls. The Earl of Caithness, who was a Sinclair too, sailed to Orkney with a Scots army, under the pretext of restoring order, although in fact covetous of the former family estates. The opposing armies had the privilege of fighting probably the only full-scale pitched battle to be witnessed on Orcadian soil—at *Summerdale* in Stenness in 1529. The Earl of Caithness was slain and his army soundly beaten. Not wishing to invoke any appeal to Denmark by Orkney, the then sixteen-year-old King James V of Scotland did not retaliate: in fact James Sinclair was knighted, installed as tacksman, and had considerable properties bestowed on him. Further concessions to Orkney included a personal visit by the King, and, under Mary Queen of Scots, the parliamentary ratification of its ancient Norse laws in 1567: but the darkest days were still to come. . . .

THE STEWART EARLS

Early Scottish government was punctuated with tyranny in Orkney, but without doubt the most notorious malefactors were the Stewart earls. Lord Robert Stewart, illegitimate son of King James V, received in 1564 the grant of lands in Orkney and Shetland from his half-sister, Mary Queen of Scots. Treasonable dealings with the King of Denmark and other disreputable activities, however, led to his imprisonment in Linlithgow for several years: but he was a wily villain, and by 1581 had not only been set free but created Earl of Orkney for good measure.

Both he and his son, Earl Patrick—or 'Black Pate', brought with them all of the evils of the feudal system. They may have been men of considerable culture, but they nevertheless rode roughshod and ruthlessly over the old odal laws and traditions. Earl Patrick was responsible for the first recorded Orcadian witchcraft prosecution, when Alison Balfour of Stenness was burnt at Gallow Hill, Kirkwall in 1594. Many more such acts of legalised barbarism were to follow, and—lest it be forgotten—constituted a most expedient method of acquiring the property—escheat, *ipso facto*—of persons so accused and convicted.

During the following centuries superstition and sorcery were to stalk the land, and many sailors shunned the Orkney Islands for the sinister powers they reputedly harboured. The full catalogue of the Stewarts' infamy cannot be related here, but another attendant evil of their rule was the widespread use and abuse of forced labour, dearly extracted from an unwilling populace, especially in the quarrying and trans-portation of stone—most of which was consigned to the construction of Earl Robert's Palace in Birsay and Earl Patrick's in Kirkwall.

Earl Patrick was arrested for treason in 1609, and was taken to Edinburgh. All might have been well for him, but he took the desperate step of sending his son, Robert, to Orkney to raise an army and recover his confiscated lands. Robert landed in Orkney in May 1614, and, surprisingly, found little difficulty in gathering support with the assis-tance of his mother. He rallied his army at Birsay, then marched on Kirkwall, capturing the castle and two palaces without opposition. Eventually, an expeditionary force sailed from Edinburgh, armed with cannon from the castle there and led by Earl George of Caithness, whose ancestor had suffered the ultimate humiliation at Summerdale. Both he and Robert Stewart were singularly inept soldiers: Robert, with his army of 500 men, could well have overwhelmed George's dimin-utive as it landed. Instead, he fired a few haphazard shots at it, then retired. He emerged again to inspect the enemy, and, thinking it too strong, retreated hastily to barricade himself and his dwindling suppor-ters (many by now had left, when they realised what poor stuff their leader was made of) in the cathedral tower, the palace and Sinclair Castle. Meanwhile George hauled his cannon to Weyland, north of Kirkwall, and on the 21st of August began his bombardment. Within several days the cannon were brought closer and soon wreaked havoc on the cathedral tower and the palace. The remaining sixteen rebels took shelter in the castle, which was so strong that bombardment continued for several weeks with little result. Earl George, complain-ing about its impregnability, wrote: "...cannon bullets broken like golf balls upon the castle, and cloven in twa haffs." With only half a barrel of powder left, a breach was eventually made in the wall; but it was the treachery of Robert's chief advisor, Patrick Halcro, that delivered him into Earl George's hands. Robert was taken to Edinburgh and executed for treason. Five weeks later, on Monday, 6th February 1614 (prior to the reformation of the calendar in 1752 the New Year began on Lady Day, i.e. 25th March) his father followed him for the same crime.

Bishop Law, who observed and documented the siege of Kirkwall Castle, performed a further service to posterity by dissuading Earl George from blowing up the cathedral in an act of retribution. The fall of Kirkwall Castle, however, sounded the last trump for any Orcadian aspirations to exist as a separate entity from Scotland.

POSTSCRIPT

The remaining history of these northern isles has little in common with that of their mainland landlord during the next two centuries—with regard, at least, to those well-told and sorry tales of religious conflict and dynastic bloodshed which loom to large in the Scottish imagination.

The zealous convictions and internecine wrangling of the Covenanters and their opponents failed to engender much enthusiasm north of the Pentland Firth. True, Montrose recruited an undisciplined army of 2,000 Orcadian farm-hands in 1650, during his last campaign for King Charles (this ended in a disastrous rout at Carbisdale, Sutherland), but not one of Orkney's leading citizens joined his cause. Thereafter Cromwell established a garrison in Orkney, but its occupation was without event. Indeed, the only notable military result was the introduction of improved gardening methods amongst Orcadians by the troops.

The Jacobite rebellions of 1715 and 1745 were fanned to life by wild, dark flames that were later to scorch the very life and soul of Gaeldom beyond repair; but few fires were kindled in Orkney. Although some lairds and merchants declared their sympathy and support for the Jacobite cause, and not a few glasses were raised in private to its success, little else transpired. Even so, after the bloody massacre and defeat of the Scots at Culloden, a few 'fireside' Jacobites in Orkney had their homes burnt for their trouble, and some proscribed citizens took up residence in the *Gentlemen's Cave* on Westray, where they bided their time till the hue and cry had died down.

The Reformation eventually made a clean sweep in Orkney, and today the Protestant faith is (to paraphrase an expression) built in with the masonry. Nowhere, however, does one meet with the ardent Calvinism typical of some of Scotland's Western Isles.

Although many stirring and historic episodes have been enacted in these deceptively peaceful islands—islands which once resounded and echoed with the clash of sagas, and in which on occasion one can almost discern whisper and footfall of dark, mysterious cultures long since vanished, its present-day inhabitants are an eminently practical, up-and-doing race with their feet firmly planted in the here and now and a weather eye on the morrow—as befits an energetic farming people with neither time nor inclination to indulge in romantic retrospection.

The Land

ORKNEY AND SHETLAND are often lumped together in the collective mind, but in reality they are as different in many respects as chalk and cheese. While Shetlanders have been described as 'fishermen with ploughs', Orcadians are first and last a farming people—around 34 per cent of total male employment emanates directly from agriculture. This agricultural tradition was established more than 5,000 years ago by neolithic Man. The friable, sandy soil of Orkney's bays and Northern Isles was well suited for cultivation—even with the primitive implements of those first settlers, who kept sheep and cattle in addition. This wealth of fertile land, incidentally, derived from the glacial deposits of clay which combined with Orkney's sandstone bedrock.

Modern land-tenure, however, with its emphasis on freehold, stems from the old Norse *odal* or *udal* system: When land passed from the first generation to the next it became 'odal', or absolutely possessed. Even so, it could not be used for such transactions as payment of a dowry or blood-money until six successive generations of possession had elapsed. At the death of an odaller his land was divided equally amongst his sons: a later amendment to odal law granted a half share to any daughters. This system encouraged the creation of many, increasingly uneconomic, small farms—a problem which was to plague Orkney for a long time to come. Odal land extended from low-water, if it was bounded by sea, to the highest stone of the highest hill and into the earth to indefinite depth. One legacy of the odal system is that shores in Orkney are not Crown property, and may be fenced. Also any claim to treasure-trove an odal land could be difficult to establish.

By the 18th century farming land was a confused conglomerate of runs, rigs, fields and strips which were usually too small to be efficient or profitable, and were frequently unenclosed, leaving crops at the mercy of wandering stock. Reform of land division was attempted around 1760, but the Orkney farmer's insistence on a slice of every cake defeated any advantage which might have accrued. It was not until the mid-19th century that land tenure and division was reformed in a viable manner, by estate owners who had taken notice of agricultural advances in the south.

Before this farming was inefficient and primitive. Only two crops were grown to any extent—bere (a form of barley) and oats. Drainage, manuring and systematic crop rotation were rarely practised. Yields were poor and the genus of seed sown had not improved since the Stone Age. The single-stilt Orkney plough was a crude and ineffectual contraption. Stock was small in size, low milk and meat yielding, and the shortage of winter feed required most of it to be slaughtered in the autumn. (The short-tailed, seaweed-eating sheep of North Ronaldsay are the only surviving relics of those days.) In the 17th and 18th centuries famines were recorded, and many people died as a consequence. But such is the quality of Orkney soil that, despite the farming methods employed, there was usually sufficient grain to export some of it, although this benefited landlord rather than tenant.

Oatmeal and beremeal were formerly the staple diet in Orkney, made into porridge and bread. Cabbage, turnips and potatoes were also grown. Most homes kept a cow for milk, butter and cheese. Beer was brewed in the winter, and to this day a strong tradition of home-brewing lives on. A pig and a few hens were usually kept, and fish frequently graced the table.

The average country farmhouse was a long, low affair, drystone built,

TOP Haymaking at Birsay circa. 1900: *Kirkwall Library.*
BOTTOM Harrowing with a 'Sheltie'—the hardy Shetland pony: *Kirkwall Library.*

35

TOP Cutting peats in the early 1900s. Similar scenes may be witnessed even today: *Kirkwall Library*. BOTTOM Carting peat by ox-power on Hoy around the turn of the century: *Kirkwall Library*.

with a thatch or flagstone roof. Indeed, many old houses are still roofed in this manner. Furniture was basic and frequently fashioned from stone. (The Orkney straw-backed chair was another manifestation of wood shortage.) Peat was the principal source of heating, and remains much in use today, although less so than formerly. Smoke from the free-standing fireplace found its exit through a hole in the roof, as did much of the heat. Light entered by the same route and windows were rare. The byre was often an extension of the house, and access to the latter was usually via the former—man and beast lived side by side. In some instances byre and barn flanked the farmhouse, with a narrow passage running between, effectively sheltering the house from the worst effects of wind and weather. There are still some quite well-preserved examples of old Orkney farmhouses, such as **Winksetter, Midhouse** and **Bimbister.**

The collapse of the kelp industry in 1832 encouraged a renewed interest in profitable farming and caused an injection of investment and new ideas. Improved communications with the south and the green revolution taking place there speeded the process. Orkney had always been a fertile land and the application of new methods made it one of the leading agricultural counties in Scotland by the end of the 19th century. In Shapinsay, for instance, 700 acres were cultivated in 1848: by 1863 6,000 acres were under the plough.

London, by the way, has a debt of gratitude to Orkney... Prior to the Reformation the Church had achieved title to virtually half Orkney's estates and lands. This ecclesiastical accumulation was subsequently sold, and, by the mid-19th century, came into the possession of the British Board of Woods and Forests. They duly disposed of this doubtful asset—an Orkney branch manager would have had much in common with the gentleman who reputedly registered with the Department of Employment in Kirkwall as a lumberjack—and the proceeds were utilised to improve the amenity of London's parks—notably by the planting of trees in Hyde Park.

At the beginning of the 19th century thirty-three proprietors owned over 90 per cent of the Orkney Islands. However, with the passing of the *Crofter's Act* in 1886 many smallholders were given security of tenure, and with this new-found commodity were heartened to make improvements to land and property. In the 1920s economic conditions led many major land-owners to sell their estates at low prices, and once again the Orkney farmer resumed the position of the odaller of old.

Today most of Orkney's three thousand or so farms are family owned and managed. The average size is thirty-five acres, although many exceed this, and 25 per cent run to ninety acres and more. Cattle-rearing is the primary activity; the familiar, black Aberdeen Angus the principal breed (although others are beginning to make headway); and Friesians and Ayrshires the backbone of the dairy industry: Altogether there are around 100,000 head of cattle throughout the Islands, and beef production is on the increase—nearly 30,000 beasts are sent south for fattening each year. Although sheep-farming is slightly on the decline at present, similar numbers of sheep are also exported; pig-farming, on the other hand, is virtually moribund. With the emphasis on stock prduction, the main crop grown in the Islands is grass—with some oats, barley, seed potatoes (which are particularly disease-free, thanks to the climate) and turnips besides.

The origin of Orkney's renowned dairy industry is worthy of mention: It took shape during World War II in order to meet the needs of thousands of troops stationed in the Islands, and, after the war, the Ministry of Food provided a factory to process the surplus milk into butter and cheese. The Milk Marketing Board took this over in 1951, and 4 million gallons are now processed annually. A remarkable egg exporting industry sprang up in like manner, and at its peak during post-war years exported some 70 million eggs annually, worth up to £1.25 million in the late 1950s. Unfortunately, this has almost completely died away.

Old ways are rapidly disappearing as larger, mechanised farms develop, and as a consequence many workers are leaving the land—particularly in the outer islands. But a few stalwarts soldier on undaunted: The tale is told of one veteran crofter (locally dubbed 'Boxing Bill') who stubbornly adheres to the ways of his forefathers, and leaves his cattle unfenced, to wander foot-loose and fancy-free... much to the chagrin of his progressive neighbours.

On a less happy note, even as this book goes to press the Orcadian farming community faces a major and totally unforseen crisis. Between August 1978 & 9 an unprecedented 51 inches of rain effectively reduced the islands' arable acreage to unworkable quagmire and swamp. Virtually half of both years' hay harvest was lost, and the result of two successive years of disasterous shortfall was total depletion of reserve winter feed-stocks—essential to the survival of Orkney's herds, most of which spend their winters indoors—and the prospect of huge bills for expensively shipped-in hay. Many farmers were left with no alternative but to sell off not just a few head of cattle, but breeding cows and even entire herds at low, loss-making prices. For some it represents a final farewell to the land. For those who survive, and Orkney in general, it is a severe blow—from which it may take years to recover.

A land of elemental beauty, it would seem, can only too easily suffer elemental ruin.

The Sea

MOST ORCADIANS have good reason to regard that Protean bearer of riches and sorrows, the sea, with double-edged feelings.

Time and time again fresh waves of humanity, culture and sudden change have broken on these northern shores: the first primitive man in search of sanctuary and shelter; knowledge of bronze and iron; the dark, arcane Pict; the frail lamp of faith carried by gentle, but determined Celtic *Papas*; land-hungry Norse settlers and magnificent, but bloody Vikings; Scottish earls, lairds and merchants; trading ships and whalers; droves of bustling herring boats; war fleets and battalions of British servicemen; North Sea oilmen; and last, but not least—the tourist. The fires that have kept Orkney's melting pot bubbling for five millennia show no signs of going out.

When the Norse came to Orkney they brought with them a tradition of seafaring which was never to be forgotten. Although they carved a posterity for themselves in Orkney's soil, they did not turn their backs on the sea. In the spring of each year the jarls who could afford the expense launched their lithe, sinuous longships, and went *a-viking,* spreading in their wake a trail of despoilation and terror round Britain's coasts and beyond. They returned for the harvest and winter—a season usually spent in carousing and listening to ballads glorifying their exploits, composed by their *skalds.*

Orkney has always relied on trading for the provision of such essentials as timber and implements, but during the 18th century these northern Isles assumed a new importance to British commerce: The pirate infested state of the English Channel and England's frequent hostilities with France persuaded many traders to risk the chartless Northabout Route for the first time, and—in so doing—established Orkney on the trading routes of Europe and America. Orkney profited greatly from the re-routing of the North American rice trade during Britain's Seven Years War with France, but this declined upon termination of hostilities in 1763, and in 1775 ceased altogether at the outbreak of the American War of Independence. However, Orkney's real shipping fortunes were still to come.

In 1760 the Davis Straits whaling ships called at **Stromness** for the first time, and took on provisions and men. This relationship lasted and enrichened Orkney until the mid-19th century, when whaling went into a decline due to ruthless hunting and subsequent reduction of whale stocks, although it was to linger on in Orkney up to the onset of World War I.

Similarly, from 1690 to 1891, the west-bound trading ships of The Hudson's Bay Company became a regular sight in Stromness. Every summer they dropped anchor here before setting sail for America; the merchants of Stromness flourished and the town grew apace; the Company found Orcadians to be willing and able workers (and cheap to hire) and up to seventy were taken on at a time—at one point seventy-five per cent of the Company's employees in Canada were Orcadian! Some rose to eminence in its service, becoming governors and explorers of note. Amongst the latter ranked Dr John Rae, who successfully led an expedition to discover the fate of Sir John Franklin's fatal expedition of 1845. (Franklin provisioned his ships *Erebus* and *Terror* in Stromness before his voyage to seek the North-West Passage—there is a plaque at the now disused *Logan's Well* in Stromness which records Franklin's connection with the town, along with that of The Hudson's Bay Company and Captain Cook, whose ships *Resolution* and *Discovery* called there in 1780.) It is said that the town's link with the Hudson's Bay Company was responsible for some North American Indian blood in Stromness.

Many ships were lost in storms around Orkney's hazardous coasts— not all of them accidentally: The wrecker's lamp shone enticingly from not a few of Orkney's cliffs, and some ministers even went so far as to invoke the Almighty to deliver such wrecks He in His infinite wisdom judged fit onto the rocks of their particular parish. This perilous state of affairs could not last forever, and in 1750 Murdoch Mackenzie produced a complete set of charts of Orkney's waters. A Lighthouse Board was established in 1786, and a series of beacons erected—the first on North Ronaldsay, an island which had claimed many shipwrecks.

Smuggling was a respectable occupation in 18th-century Orkney, and

The Sneuk, Hoy by William Daniell, R.A.

many a family founded its fortunes on free trade with Norway, Germany and France. At this time the press gangs were busy too, and such was the demand for sailors—both willing and unwilling—that the female population of Stromness at one stage was almost double that of the male. However, undoubtedly the most picaresque event in the annals of maritime freebooting in the Orkneys concerns piracy.

John Gow was born in Caithness in 1690 and spent his childhood in Stromness. As a youth he ran away to sea, and for a while earned the excellent reputation most Orcadian sailors were worthy of. However, in time he was to lead a mutiny, murdering his officers and assuming command of his ship. For a few months he terrorised Britain's sea lanes, until he decided to return to Orkney in order to avoid the attention his depredations were attracting from His Majesty's Government. In 1725, under the guise of a merchant vessel, he sailed into Stromness and anchored at the back of the Holms.

All at first was quiet, and folk were impressed with how well the local lad had fared in the world. But the increasingly outrageous behaviour of his unruly and ruffianly crew soon raised suspicions. These were confirmed when a prisoner Gow had been holding escaped—making straight for the magistrates in Kirkwall—and some press-ganged crew made a run for it, and were picked up by Custom's men. Hastily, Gow plundered the house of William Honeyman, laird of Graemsay, in Clestrain, taking plate and a piper, then fled. He ran aground on the Calf of Cava, where—finding nothing else of value—he forced two girls aboard. Freeing his ship, he sailed to Calf Sound, Eday, and anchored, with the intention of plundering the house of James Fea of Carrick, whom he had known in his youth. However, Mr Fea had seen the warning fires which had been lit meanwhile on Wideford Hill, and, feigning friendship, outwitted and captured Gow. (A stain on the floor of Carrick House is attributed to Gow's blood.) He was handed over to the authorities, and subsequently, along with seven of his associates, hanged in Wapping's Execution Dock. As his corpse hung in chains his erstwhile Stromness lover travelled to London to clasp his hand, so undoing the binding *Oath of Odin* which they had sworn together. (q.v.) The adventures of John Gow inspired Sir Walter Scott to write his novel *The Pirate*—"...so indifferently written but so romantically conceived, for the desolate islands and roaring tideways of the North." as R.L. Stevenson was later to remark of it.

During the 19th century a flourishing fishing industry grew up in the Islands. In 1837 710 herring boats were working from Orkney, mostly based in Stronsay and Stromness. But these boats were largely operated by non-Orcadian fishermen: fishing, as a means of earning a living, was not highly thought of in Orkney, although many crofters worked small boats in their spare time.

By the late-19th century the industry had escalated to boom proportions. Most of the activity was confined to July and August, and 800 boats were recorded in Stromness one year, along with 5,000 fishermen and gutters. Spirits could run high at these times and Stromness merchants took care to shutter their shops at night (at one stage forty 'inns' were in existence in Stromness). Catches became erratic, however, and by the First World War the shoals of silver darlings had all but vanished. The great days of herring fishing were over, but the demise of the industry left a legacy of vastly improved navigational lights around Orkney.

There were no scheduled shipping connections with Scotland in the 18th century, and such links as did exist were with Leith. Quantities of beremeal and oatmeal were shipped to Norway, the West Highlands, the Netherlands, Spain, Portugal and Ireland. Returning boats brought with them timber, utensils, salt, flax and coal. The profits from this trading established a new merchant class who accumulated estates and rose in influence and power: such families were the Baikies, Traills and Craigies. During the 19th century, however, communications with mainland Scotland greatly improved, the first regular steamer service coming into operation in 1836 (summer only) from Leith via Aberdeen and Wick. This was the paddle steamer *Sovereign*. In 1861 a screw steamer commenced operating all year round.

Scapa Flow was first mapped in 1812 by the government as a proposed anchorage for British battle fleets. The strategic nature of

An Orcadian fisherman circa. 1900: *Kirkwall Library.*

FISHING BOATS LEAVING STROMNESS HARBOUR 1906. T.K.

TOP Herring fleets sailing from Stromness in 1906: *Kirkwall Library*. BOTTOM One of the many casualties claimed by Orkney's hazardous coastal waters in bygone days: *Kirkwall Library*.

44

these fifty square miles of sheltered, deep water was not lost to the High Command during two world wars either. The British Home and Atlantic Fleets were based here during World War I, and installations were built at Lyness and Longhope. Ships were scuttled in the approaches to deter submarines, and minefields and booms were laid.

The feelings of many of the men who were stationed here during the wars can be summed up in the words of Captain Hamish Blair's poem, *Bloody Orkney*. (The title is self-explanatory.) The fleets swung on their anchorages for two years with little action, and the military personnel filled their days with pointless duty activities and were encouraged to take up gardening in their free time to keep the fleet supplied with vegetables. Most men were ship based, but their large numbers must have overrun a bemused, although not entirely resentful Orkney—business had never been better.

The fleet's vegetating existence came to an abrupt end in 1916, when it put to sea to engage the German High Fleet off Jutland in the last, full-scale, pitched sea-battle ever to be fought. Both sides claimed victory. During the armistice of 1918 it was agreed that the German Fleet should be interned in Scapa to await the outcome of the peace treaty. Some eighty warships, manned by increasingly undisciplined skeleton crews, lay in the Flow. Rollerskating on the decks of the German flagship *Friedrich der Grosse* eventually drove the German Admiral to move his quarters to a more peaceful ship. Meanwhile, unknown to the British, plans to scuttle the fleet were being made by the German officers.

On May 31st 1919 the German personnel celebrated their 'German victory at Jutland', much to the chagrin of the British. On June 21st— the original deadline issued to Germany to sign the peace treaty—a small party of schoolchildren from Stromness was taken by boat to view the German Fleet. Their's was the most expensive school treat ever laid on. Before their very eyes, and accompanied by much enthusiastic clapping and cheering, the glory that was the German Fleet sank ship by ship into Scapa Flow. The few British naval personnel present managed to run one or two ships onto the shore before they were lost, but the only one of significance saved was the battleship *Baden*. All was not loss however: The rights to this naval graveyard were purchased by Ernest F.G. Cox, 'the man who bought a navy', and the ensuing salvage work created employment in Orkney during the lean years of the Depression. Some seven ships remain there, and work continues. The metal so salvaged is of particular value to scientists, as its long immersion in the sea has preserved it from nuclear contamination.

At the outbreak of World War II the British Fleet was back in Scapa Flow in force, with Churchill again in command. Scapa was not as secure as it had previously been—air attack had now to be reckoned with. German bombers struck in October 1939, holing the old battleship *Iron Duke*, which had to be run aground. One bomber was shot down and the first German prisoner-of-war captured on British soil was taken. The bombers returned in March 1940, only to be frightened off by British fighters. One bomber jettisoned its load over Bridge of Waithe, and in so doing claimed the first British civilian death of the war. Meanwhile, disaster of another kind had struck. . . .

On October 14th 1939 the German submarine *U47* demonstrated the vulnerability of the Flow, when it crept between the rusting hulks of World War I blockships in Kirk Sound, and torpedoed the mighty *Royal Oak.* Amazingly, of the first salvo of torpedoes, only one struck home and the explosion was not attributed to enemy action. Twenty minutes later any doubts were dispelled when several torpedoes hit their target. Within minutes the *Royal Oak* capsized and sank, with the loss of 809 men and 24 officers. The submarine escaped. Soon after this 5,000 workmen moved in, and a plethora of gun emplacements and other defenses was built.

Between 1941-3 Italian prisoners-of-war were deployed along with British civilians to build the **Churchill Barriers**—causeways of huge, five and ten ton concrete blocks, over which at a later date roads were built, effectively joining Burray and South Ronaldsay to Mainland. For a second time war had benefited Orkney's economy. (The Italian prisoners left another memorial behind them—**The Italian Chapel** on Lamb Holm, now a popular tourist attraction.) Such was the formidable strength of anti-aircraft fire power by now, that Scapa was less and less troubled by air attack. (These lethal pyrotechnics were so spectacular and costly that they became known as *Brock's Benefit.*)

During World War II up to 60,000 servicemen were stationed in Orkney—three times the indigenous population. Orkney was not the most sought after posting, but conditions for the troops were far better than they had been during the previous war. Many more were land based, and eventual facilities included electricity and hot water. Cinemas and a theatre were built, and a successful forces newspaper, *The Orkney Blast*, was founded by Eric Linklater, the famous Orkney-born novelist, then a major in the Royal Engineers.

After the dust of occupation had died down the vast amount of material and equipment abandoned by the War Department was put to good use, although not all W.D. cast-offs were welcome: To this day Orkney remains scabbed with the unlovely fabrications of war, many of which were built to withstand bombing. Unless some determined attempt to remove them is made, these reinforced concrete eyesores are liable to become as integral a part of the landscape as Orkney's other and more venerable monuments to Man's megalithic ingenuity.

Industry

WHEN ONE THINKS of Orkney, the work 'industry' is not one which springs readily to mind. Dark satanic mills have no place here, but industry, nonetheless, there is—and was: strangely enough, one of the major contributory factors towards the development of Orkney's economy was the collapse of what was once a lucrative industry in these Islands.

Certain types of seaweed, when burnt, produce a liquid which solidifies on cooling: this substance was formerly an essential ingredient in soap production, bleaching and glass manufacturing. It was extracted from Orkney kelp and exported for around £20 per ton by estate-owners between 1720 and 1832. Revenue from this helped significantly in keeping many estates profitable: thus, when import duty on barilla, a cheap foreign substitute, was removed in 1832, estate-owners were once again obliged to look to their lands for income. The result was rapid and revolutionary improvements to Orcadian agriculture, long overdue. Many old kelp-burning pits can still be seen scattered around Orkney's shores.

In more recent times new enterprises have developed which, fortunately, show no signs of sharing the same fate; in fact, quite the reverse. Principal amongst these is distilling.

There are two whisky distilleries in Orkney, both in the vicinity of Kirkwall. *Scapa Distillery*, founded in 1885, is the least well known of the two, as most of its product goes to blending. *Highland Park*, on the other hand, is something of a household word. This distillery, founded in

47

1795, bottles its own product at various degrees of proof and age, and it is easily obtainable. At its highest degrees of proof it is said to compare with the finest brandy. Highland Park's pot still is the largest in Scotland, and during World War II its mash-tuns were utilised as communal baths for servicemen. The distillery stands on the former site of a bothy, where lived Magnus Eunson, a church officer and the greatest and most accomplished smuggler in Orkney's history. He kept his illicit spirit under the pulpit of a nearby church, and on one occasion he received word that the church was to be searched by excisemen. The kegs were removed to his bothy, a coffin lid placed over them, and a white sheet over that. When the excisemen arrived, Eunson and his confederates were on their knees with prayer books, singing a psalm for the dead. The word 'small-pox' was whispered, and the trustees of legal liquor vanished hastily into the night... the devil, as they say, has all the best tunes!

The essential ingredient of Highland park—water— is unique in being pumped up from wells below the distillery, which is built on a hill. That apart, tradition thrives here, the original floor-maltings being still in use and peat being cut from the distillery's own peat-beds. A little heather is added to the peat used to dry the malt, giving the whisky a unique flavour. Both distilleries may be visited by previous appointment.

Although tourism is still very much a secondary consideration in Orkney—unlike some areas of Scotland—it nevertheless contributes in no small way to the economy of the Islands. The 'industry', which it most certainly is today, began in the 1880s with round trips by steam boat from Leith and Aberdeen. In 1894 a cruise taking in Kirkwall, the Fair Isle, Foula and Lerwick was advertised for £5. Although prices have risen slightly since then, the number of visitors continues to grow yearly; nevertheless, it is perhaps unfortunate that so many restrict themselves to the Mainland-South Ronaldsay group, when the outlying Islands are so worthy of attention.

Although Shetland is more readily associated with knitting, the craft has long been a traditional activity in Orkney. Only fairly recently, however, has it developed the status of an industry, with many home-workers knitting for agencies, which in turn market the goods in Europe and America. Much is machine-made, although lovely, hand-made items of traditional design can still be found. The *Sanday Knitters Association* is a prominent name, and is one of several workers co-operatives.

Fishing is another relatively small, but developing industry in Orkney. The bulk of it is based on lobster fishing, although crabs and clams are much sought. Until recently crabs were thrown back into the sea, but new processing plants in Westray, Rousay, Kirkwall and

The graceful lines of a traditional clinker-built lobster-boat drawn up in one of the many nousts which serrate the Stromness waterfront. The lighthouse supply ship *Pole Star* is visible in the background.

TOP Pot stills at Highland Park Distillery, Kirkwall.
BOTTOM Storage tanks at the Occidental Oil terminal on Flotta: *Loganair*.

Stromness extract the meat, which is sold in frozen blocks in Britain and Europe. White fishing is a recent development too, with many new boats of up to 75ft. catching cod, haddock, skate, etc. Stromness is the centre of Orkney's fishing industry, and there is an *Orkney Fishermen's Society* based there.

With its Norse heritage, it is hardly surprising that there is a thriving boat-building industry in Orkney. The style of local craft has more than a hint of Norse ancestry in its lines to boot. There are over half-a-dozen boat yards in Orkney producing the venerable clinker-built dinghy, light but resilient, as well as larger fishing boats, mostly in wood, although there is one very successful GRP yard in Kirkwall. Another yard has continued in the same family for five generations.

Less traditional, perhaps, but equally successful is a small electronics factory on Sanday which has produced such items as a language laboratory for Hong Kong and communications training equipment for a Middle Eastern Government... Orkney is full of surprises!

Craft industries are undergoing a revival, and there are now a considerable number of people in Orkney producing articles, useful, attractive, or both. There are two silversmithing businesses in Kirkwall manufacturing jewellery on a relatively large scale, besides several individual workers in the Islands. Sheepskins are widely cured, dressed and produced as rugs; there are several potteries; and the traditional straw-backed Orkney chair can still be purchased. Other crafts include sealskin goods, wrought ironwork and woodturning.

One business in Kirkwall imports salmon from North America to produce *Orkney Smoked Salmon*, the process being a closely guarded family secret. This delicacy has graced the tables of the Royal Family, prime ministers and millionaires, has satisfied the egalitarian appetites of Russian premiers, and is regularly despatched to such exotic destinations as Hong Kong, Moscow, Vienna, Paris and Dar-es-Salaam. The same firm can boast the distinction of having been elevated '...into the place and quality of Cheesemonger' to the Queen Mother, and having been awarded the unique accolade in Orkney of *Royal Warrant Holder*.

There are many more such tales of successful individual enterprise, and many other small businesses too numerous to mention, but the emphasis is definitely on family concerns. Orcadian financial acumen is highly regarded outwith the Islands: trading is woven into the fabric of Orkney life, and it has produced a breed of remarkably shrewd businessmen and women, not easily outdone in the market-place.

In recent years Britain's northern isles have become vital bases for the oil exploration and production industries. Shetland, perhaps, is more dramatically affected, but oil is a topic of conversation almost as popular in Orkney as the weather, and as frequently praised and damned. Every week *The Orcadian* carries another front-page story about it; hooded parkas (the oilman's uniform) are seen everywhere in the streets; aircraft land and take off with increasing frequency; supply ships and tenders of assorted nationality sail in and out of Stromness and Kirkwall harbours; business is brisk, and there is an unquestionable injection of money into Orkney's economy (Orkney's annual revenue from oil currently runs well in excess of £1 million). But there are the usual inevitable tensions—not everyone is happy. There is, for example, concern about oil spillage, although to date only a few minor spills have occurred, which, fortunately, were promptly dealt with.

An international consortium attempted to obtain permission to build concrete oil-rigs in Houton Bay, and met with total public opposition— not on principle, but rather due to their approach; i.e., throwing money about with promises of good things to come—not a propitious wooing technique in Orkney, especially with the debris of two world wars still painfully obvious.

However, the principal extent of Orkney's commitment to oil at present is well out of sight, and consists of Occidental's storage terminal on *Flotta*. The farm of Whanclett was flattened to make way for seven huge storage tanks, which now retain the oil piped from the *Piper* and *Claymore* fields until leviathan super-tankers call to ship it away.

Perhaps a more sensitive word than *oil* in Orkney is **uranium**....A deposit of uranium ore has been discovered near Stromness, and the threat of the creation of an open-cast mine recently occasioned two of the few demonstration marches ever witnessed in Orkney. No doubt if the government of the day decides that it is in 'the national interest' to extract it, then nothing will prevent it—although, should this transpire, it will be in the face of virtually 100 per cent local opposition. Whether Orkney likes it or not, the 20th century, with its concomitant energy demands, is knocking at the door. Ironically, some islands are still without mains electricity supply.

The canny Orcadian, however, lives in a land where invasion— whether human, economic, or both—is not a new experience, and coping with it, adapting to it, and turning it to advantage are well learnt skills. They show no signs of falling into disrepair.

Superstitions & Customs

ORKNEY'S COLLECTIVE IMAGINATION was once rich in superstitious belief, much of it based on Norse mythology and interwoven with the rituals of work and daily life. Trolls, dwarfs, elves and brownies inhabited the hills and mounds, and the sea teemed with monsters, mermaids and *Finmen*. The sea was the domain of the dreadful *Stoor Worm*, the world serpent whose coils encircled the earth. Traditionally he was slain by a young farmhand named Assipattle. Serpents and monsters appear frequently in Orkney's sea-lore, and as recently as 1910 a sighting of a creature with a neck 18 feet long was attested to in Shapinsay Sound by three witnesses. One particularly repulsive denizen of the deep was known as *Nuckellavee*, and his presence on land was often held responsible for blight, drought or pestilence. Mermaids were less malignant, and in the 1890s a creature known as the *Deerness Mermaid* was sighted by hundreds of people in Newark Bay. Such fishy ladies and their male counterparts, Finmen, were said to inhabit the legendary *Finfolkaheem*, their enchanted and enchanting kingdom at the bottom of the ocean. In summer they moved to *Hildaland*, a lush and beautiful island. (This was the old name for Eynhallow.) Tales of seal people or *selchies* are common. They often involved a seal woman, stranded in her mortal coils by the purloining of her seal skin, marrying the unsuspected culprit. Years later she discovers her seal skin and, donning it, returns to the sea and her true love. Occasionally the seal-creature takes male form, and inexplicable fecundity on the part of a country lass was sometimes attributed to a seal-man. This is the theme of *The Selchie of*

Sule Skerry ballad.

The trolls and trows who were believed to stalk the countryside at night, doing mischief, and abducting women, children and cattle, were a legacy of Norse culture. Considerable precautions were taken against them, especially at Yule when they were most dangerous. Another mound-dweller was the *hogboy* or *hogboon*, usually the tutelary spirit of a house or farm who inhabited a nearby tumulus. Offerings of milk and ale were made to him, and even the occasional sacrifice, ensuring the continued success of man, beast and harvest. Belief in this creature long discouraged interference with and investigation into Orkney's many cairns, from the certain, dire consequences which would result.

Belief in witchcraft can be traced back to Norse times in Orkney, but such witchcraft was usually healing and beneficial. Nevertheless, both Orkney and Shetland were given a wide berth by many sailors as late as the 19th century for their supernatural reputation. The first half of the 17th century was notorious for witch-hunts and burnings. Many hapless creatures perished on Gallow Hill near Kirkwall; 'taking the profit' from a neighbour's cow was a common allegation. The witch's powers extended to command of weather and sea, and up to the end of the 19th century sailors could still buy fair winds and calm seas. Such sway over the elements was not taken lightly, for the ability some old crones had to cause storms was well known. At Mill Bay in Stronsay, a storm witch known as Scota Bess weaved her maledictions from an embrasure in the crags called 'The Maiden's Chair.' The gifts of foresight and knowledge are said to be bestowed on any girl who sits there.

Frequent reference is made in Orcadian folklore to *The Book of the Black Arts*. This was printed white on black and possession of a copy conferred magic powers on its owner. If one died with it in one's possession, however, both book and one's soul were claimed by the dark one. One could only dispose of the book by selling it for smaller coin than was paid for it, or by giving it away. Obviously this became progressively more difficult. A Sandwick man reputedly tried to dispose of his copy of this fiendish publication by heaving it overboard his boat, weighted with stones. When he returned home it was to find the book on the kitchen table, dry as ever. A Sanday girl, who had unwittingly accepted a copy from a local witch, tried by every means imaginable to rid herself of it—to no avail. According to local legend, these unfortunates were rescued from the probable exercise of diabolic preemption only thanks to the intervention of the Reverend Charles Clouston (died 1884) and the Reverend Matthew Armour (died 1903), who disposed of the respective copies.

The *Stone of Odin* which once stood at Stenness was pulled down in 1814. It had a hole in it through which lovers would clasp hands, swear undying love for each other, and then repeat the now forgotten *Oath of*

Odin. The stone was also credited with healing and restorative powers. The **Ring of Brogar** was once known as the Temple of the Sun, and the **Stones of Stenness** as the Temple of the Moon. It is said that after New Year celebrations and feasting at Stenness Kirk, young lovers would slip away to pray to Woden, first at the Stenness Stones, where the girl would pray, and then at Brogar, where the man would pray—then together make the Oath of Odin.

Thunder Stones were smooth stones or polished neolithic axe-heads which were believed to be bringers of good luck and protection against lightning. They are still found now and again, lodged in the chimneys of old houses.

Several wells and springs in Orkney are held to have magical healing properties. The well of Kindinguie is mentioned elsewhere (q.v. *Stronsay*). The contents of the well at Bigswell, Stenness were considered to be particularly efficacious at Beltane and Midsummer; the well to be first circled clockwise before the waters were drunk. The mentally afflicted required more intensive treatment—they were ducked in the well, then left all night tied up to a post beside it! Certain venerable religious sites were also sought out by pilgrims in search of a cure. Such were the chapels of **St Tredwell (Papa Westray)**, Cleat (Sanday), Lady Kirk (South Ronaldsay), and the chapels at the Broughs of Birsay and Deerness. Usually a small oblation was left.

There is a tradition surrounding *heather ale* in Orkney. (The secret of its brewing supposedly vanished with the Picts.) Robert Louis Stevenson immortalised it in one of his poems.

Much superstition was attached to ploughing and the horse. A confraternity known as *The Horsemen* conducted many cabbalistic rites, rituals and initiations associated with these concomitant institutions. The antecedents of this society are obscure, lost in the mists of time: its former adherents frequently believed that their special powers conferred on them mastery over woman as well as horse. As a society it still exists—hopefully with modified views!

South Ronaldsay boasts a number of attested hauntings. In Matthew's Glen the spectral figures of an old man and woman have reputedly been seen. At Kirkhouse a woman walks along a passage holding a foot under each arm—it is said to be the ghost of a dairymaid who claimed herself to have seen apparitions in a graveyard, and swore to the veracity of her tale with the injunction: 'May my feet go rotten and drop off if it isn't true!' She contracted a disease and died of gangrene.

At the ruined farm of Nether Benzieclett, Sandwick, where a king of Norway is reputed to have slept, a spectral grey ewe is said to appear at 1 a.m. every morning in the ale cupboard, where a man was murdered. In similar vein, tradition has it that a spectral dog on occasion suddenly appears to travellers from beneath the bridge at Quholmsley near Stromness, follows them for a little distance, then disappears. Several disasters are said to have occurred in the neighbourhood.

The vicinity of Clestrain, overlooking Graemsay, is also said to be haunted. In 1758 the laird of Graemsay, William Honeyman (who was robbed by John Gow, the pirate), made a trading voyage to the Hebrides, leaving a considerable sum of money and jewellery buried near a dyke, which he charged to the care of his wife, Mary. He never returned, although a spectral ship was seen to sail into his anchorage and vanish. A later report confirmed that both he and his ship had been lost in a storm. His wife died soon afterwards; and during the next century a lady clad in white was frequently reported as having been seen walking near the dyke where the treasure had been buried. (This has never been found, despite repeated attempts to locate it.)

The eternal promise of seed, soil and the seasons—a *sine qua non* of agriculture, formerly shot through and hedged about with ritual—is still recalled each year in South Ronaldsay by the *Festival of the Horse* and *Boys' Ploughing Match*. Held now in mid-August for the benefit of tourists, it originally took place in the spring. The boys of the district assemble on the *Sands O'Right* near St Margaret's Hope, and armed with miniature ploughs—usually finely wrought and treasured family heirlooms—plough furrows in the wet sand which are subsequently judged for straightness and evenness. The little girls—and some of the smaller boys—rig themselves up as 'horses', complete with simulated tails, fetlocks, collars, bridles, etc., and bedecked and festooned with anything bright, gay or glittering which can be pressed into service. The day ends with tea, games, prize-giving and dancing. The roots of the custom are uncertain.

No account of Orcadian customs would be complete without mention of the renowned *Ba' Game*—Orkney's answer to the playing fields of Eton. Twice yearly, once at Christmas and once at the New Year, the streets of Kirkwall become the scene of a more or less bloodless battle between two teams—the *Uppies* and the *Doonies*—with up to 150 men or boys participating. The object of the 'game' is the propulsion of a leather ball to either end of the town by whatever tactics necessary. Once there, the game is won. Should the Doonies prevail, the game usually ends on a damp note... their goal is the harbour. The stramash can last for hours, with scrums forming, breaking and re-forming up and down the main streets and closes. The origins of the game are obscure, although some say it is a relic of Norse leisure activities; others, that Kirkwall got the notion from the treatment its citizens meted out to the severed head of a vanquished and hated enemy. The basis for the teams is indisputably the enmity which existed between the Bishop's men

TOP Boys' Ploughing Match on the Sands O'Right, St. Margaret's Hope: *Phoenix Photos*. BOTTOM The Ba' Game, Kirkwall: *Phoenix Photos*.

Domestic occupations before the Age of Leisure—TOP Spinning yarn on Shapinsay &
grinding meal by hand-quern: *Kirkwall Library*. BOTTOM Making a traditional Orkney
straw-backed chair: *Kirkwall Library*.

(Uppies) and the Earl's men (Doonies) in the 16th century and before.

In days past the Orkney calendar was enriched with the observance of many more festivals than is the case today. Such were the Yule celebrations, which lasted for many days; the Johnmas bonfires, with much dancing around them; and the once most important event of the year—the Lammas Fair in Kirkwall. The New Year, however, is still celebrated in heroic fashion; and every year, on the island of Hoy in the parish of the same name, the arrival of Midsummer is signalised by a large Solstice bonfire. The more energetic of those present generally ascend the summit of Ward Hill to greet the dawn.

Historic Monuments &
Places of Interest

THE FOLLOWING GAZETTEER lists and describes the principal monuments, etc. located in Orkney, besides some which are not so well known. Of necessity many secondary archaeological sites are not given here—there are altogether in excess of 1,000 within these Islands.

For this reason, the reader is advised to obtain a good map or maps to supplement this book. The 1:50,000 map series published by the Ordnance Survey is recommended: it covers the Northern Isles *(sheet 5)*, Mainland *(sheet 6)*, and the Southern Isles *(sheet 7— Pentland Firth)*. These are very detailed and well worth the expense. Bartholomew's Half-Inch series renders the Orkneys in their entirety on one map *(No. 61)*. This is adequate, although many sites are not indicated.

☆ ☆ ☆

Historic Monuments, etc. are numbered as indicated on the map of Orkney at the beginning of the book. The figures given in brackets [255275], etc. — are their O.S. map National Grid Reference co-ordinates *S.D.D.*, denotes that the monument is in the guardianship of the Scottish development Department. *Standard Hours* denotes that the monument is open to the public only at the following times:

April to September — Weekdays 9.30 am to 7 pm
Sundays 2 pm to 7 pm
October to March — Weekdays 9.30 am to 4 pm
Sundays 2 pm to 4 pm

☆ ☆ ☆

I am told that there are people who do not care for maps, and find it hard to believe. The names, the shapes of the woodlands, the courses of the roads and rivers, the prehistoric footsteps of man still traceable up hill and down dale, the mills and the ruins, the ponds and the ferries, perhaps the *Standing Stone* or the *Druidic Circle* on the heath; here is an inexhaustible fund of interest for any man with eyes to see or two-pence worth of imagination to understand with!

ROBERT LOUIS STEVENSON

---

1. BARONY MILL, MAINLAND [255275]
Working corn mill (1873)
Situated ½m. E of Earl's Palace, Birsay on *A967*. The last Orcadian water mill in daily use is of comparatively recent construction, but it is the last of a long line of mills in this vicinity. Both homegrown and imported grain are processed, and beremeal milled at Barony is exported to both Shetland and the Hebrides.

2. BIMBISTER, MAINLAND [329163]
Old Orkney Farmhouse (19th century)
150 yds. E of *A986*. A typical example of its type, with corn-drying oven at one end. House and barn are conjoined in integral construction.

3. BISHOP'S PALACE, KIRKWALL
(12th century) S.D.D.

60

Adjacent to St. Magnus Cathedral and of contemporaneous construction, it was much altered during the 16th century by Bishop Reid, who added the huge 'Moosie Toor' (tower) and most of what is visible today. This is little more than a rectangular shell—formerly it comprised of a large hall with a series of cellars below this. An armorial panel on the tower's NW side represents the heraldic arms of Bishop Reid: an effigy of St Olaf occupies a nearby niche. King Haakon IV of Norway died here in 1263 after his abortive campaign against the Scots and his subsequent defeat at the Battle of Largs; and it is said that Edinburgh University was founded after a council held here. The Palace has lain unused since the formal ratification of the Protestant cause in 1689 (the *Bill of Rights*), and much of its stone has been removed by local builders. (Guide in attendance. Descriptive booklet available. Entrance fee. *Standard Hours.*)

4. BLACKHAMMER CAIRN, ROUSAY [414277]
Stalled cairn, S.D.D.
This lies between two other cairns on the landward side of R's south coast road. Similar to Midhowe, but smaller, it likewise possesses double walls and a decorated outer wall. The inner chamber is 43 ft. in length, and is partitioned by seven 'stalls' down either side. The 10 ft. long entrance passage is now blocked and entrance is gained via the roof. Two interments were discovered within the chamber along with an Onston-ware bowl, a stone axe, a flint knife and tools. (Free admission. Open all times.)

5. BROUGH OF BIRSAY [235285]
Tidal island: Celtic, Pictish and Norse settlements (7th - 15th centuries), S.D.D.
Located off NW tip of Mainland, and accessible approximately between 3 hrs. after H.W. and 3 hrs. before following H.W. (H.W. Kirkwall minus 1 hr.).

Less than ½m. square, this grassy and peaceful place looms behind the tiny village of Birsay like a time-stranded whale—a diminutive enough land-swell, but one with a past of heroic proportions. From the puffin-inhabited, sheer cliffs of its seaward west coast it declines gently downhill towards the strand connecting it with Mainland on the E side. Hard by this is to be found the clue to the island's significance—a farrago of ruinous Early Christian and Norse settlements and structures. The earliest remains are those of a Celtic community: little can be discerned of the original church—it has vanished beneath later constructions—but a small churchyard, enclosed by a curved wall and containing both graves and a series of other buildings, is still evident. The discovery here of the famous 'Birsay Stone' established beyond doubt the settlement's Celtic credentials. The original stone is now in the National Museum of Antiquities in Edinburgh, but a replica has been substituted. This monument is, in fact, a Pictish symbol stone (q.v.) and carries on it the figures of three cloaked and bearded warriors in file, each bearing sword, shield and spear. Also inscribed are characteristic Pictish symbols: crescent and V-shaped rod; mirror; eagle; and a fantastic creature—the 'swimming' elephant. The building which was superimposed over the earlier Celtic monastery and chapel was the small cathedral church, Christ Church, which was built by Earl Thorfinn on his return from Rome, probably around 1050. Later modifications date from the 12th and 13th centuries. From Birsay, Thorfinn ruled Orkney, Shetland, Caithness, the Hebrides and a dominion in Ireland. He spent the last seventeen years of his dramatic life here in relative peace, and, besides Christ Church, built a small palace, which may still be identified. After Earl Magnus was declared to be a saint by Bishop William in 1135 his relics were removed from here (in the small wooden coffin which had been interred below the nave floor of Thorfinn's church—now in Tankerness House Museum) and installed as a shrine in the now vanished St Olaf's Church in Kirkwall, and, later, transferred to the cathedral dedicated to him. Thorfinn's remains were subsequently interred in their stead, within his own church—the most venerable in Orkney. Buildings to the N of Christ Church are believed to be the ruins of a 12th century palace of the bishopric. The foundations of thirteen Norse longhouses dating from the 10th and 11th centuries are also located here, complete with passages and courts—a town in its day. Further buildings are located on the seaward side of the church, and these date from a similar period, although much reconstruction and later modification are evident. Also worthy of note on the island is a Viking boatslip near the cliff edge. Excavation work continues, and no doubt much remains to be discovered here, but it is clear that Brough of Birsay was an important and powerful settlement in its day. (Small museum on site. Descriptive booklet available. Entrance fee. Closed Mondays in winter. Custodian—G. Spence, Tel. Birsay 343. *Standard Hours.*)

Recent excavations at *Point of Buckquoy* (leading to the Brough) unearthed the remains on several dwellings of Pictish origin, dating from somewhat after A.D. 600 and inhabited for almost 300 years, as Pictish and Norse artifacts found here testify to—these being now on display in Tankerness House Museum, along with a scale model of the site.

6. CHURCHILL BARRIERS
Causeways linking South Isles to Mainland
These were constructed in the 1940s by British civilians and Italian prisoners-of-war in order to prevent enemy submarines entering Scapa Flow. A road surface was laid over the huge five and ten-ton concrete blocks at the end of the war, thereby connecting South Ronaldsay and Burray to Mainland. The remains of partly submerged blockships are still visible alongside.

7. CLICK MILL, MAINLAND [323226]
Restored corn-grinding water-mill (early 19th century), S.D.D.
Located 3m. from Dounby, near Millbridge, 200yds. from B9057. One of the very few examples of its kind in Scotland, although once common in the Orkney and Shetland Islands. The mill is situated within a small stone hut by a stream: the grinding mechanism works, and a key to turn on the water can be obtained. The mill is of relatively recent construction, but it exemplifies the earliest type of water-powered quern. The upper stone, four feet in diameter, is driven by a shaft running through the lower stone and is attached to a horizontal water-wheel beneath the floor. It is almost certainly built on the site of earlier mills, as local place-names testify. (Descriptive leaflet available. Free admission. Open all times.)

8. CUBBIE ROO'S CASTLE, WYRE [442264]
Norse keep-tower (12th century), S.D.D.
First recorded in 1150, the 'castle' stands on the summit of a ridge near the centre of the island, and was built by Kolbein Hruga—'a mighty man from Norway'—along with nearby *Wyre Chapel* (q.v.). His son, Bjarni, became Bishop of Orkney and composed the renowned *Jomsvikingadrapa*. In 1231 King Haakon's steward in Orkney, Hanef, withstood siege here against followers of Earl John of Orkney and Caithness after murdering him in a cellar in Thurso. The term 'Cubbie Roo' derives from *Kubbe* or *Kobbe*, Norse sobriquets for Kolbein. Although the keep now stands only eight feet high, entrance was originally gained via a door at first floor level. The whole is surrounded by a defensive ditch and earthwork. The nearby *Bu* was almost certainly the site of Kolbein's homestead. (Free admission. Open all times.)

9. CUWEEN CAIRN, MAINLAND [364128]
Early chambered cairn, S.D.D.
1m. SE of Finstown, 500yds. from road. Although Cuween is not dissimilar to Maeshowe it is not so ambitious. Entrance is gained via a 17½ft. long passage, the last 10ft. of which are roofed to a height of only 2½ft., the outer portion being unroofed. The rectangular main chamber measures 11ft. x 5½ft. and rises to 7½ft. The roof is of recent construction since the chamber was originally broached via this route, as with Maeshowe. Four corbelled mural cells lead off the inner chamber. When entered in 1901 it was found to contain eight inhumations; five skulls on the floor of the main chamber and others in the s and w mural cells; and some long bones, slightly burnt. Amongst animal bones discovered were those of ox, horse, dog,

birds and two dozen dog's skulls. The external diameter of the tumulus is 55ft. (Free admission. *Standard Hours.*)

10. DWARFIE STONE, HOY [244005]
Rock-cut tomb (3rd or 4th millennium B.C.), S.D.D.
Set in desolate moorland below Ward Hill, 400yds. from Rackwick Road. It consists of a huge block of sandstone, 28ft. long, 13ft. deep and up to 7ft. high, into which runs a narrow passage, 7½ft. long. At the end of this are two small chambers, one on either side. The smaller of the two and part of the passage were formerly open to the sky, having collapsed or been broken in, but this is now restored. This object was long the subject of speculation and legend, until 1935, when it was demonstrated that it was the only example of a rock-cut tomb in Britain (or rock cut **bomb** as *The Shell Guide to Scotland* would have it!), and bore relationship to the chambered cairns in its style of masonry. Since then another such tomb has been discovered at Glendalough, Co. Wicklow in Ireland. A large block of stone lying close by the entrance was obviously intended for sealing it. Sir Walter Scott immortalised it in his novel, *The Pirate.* (Free admission. Open all times.)

11. EARL'S PALACE, BIRSAY [247278]
Palace of Robert Stewart, Earl of Orkney (1574), S.D.D.
Located near the shore, in the tiny hamlet of Birsay. It is of open courtyard design and, although somewhat ruinous, possesses many architecturally interesting features, including a mosaic tile floor and towers at three corners. Restoration work is currently in progress. Numerous gun-loops are set into the towers, courtyard and north flank of the palace; this last dating from somewhat later than the rest of the building. The structure is mainly fabricated from split blocks and lime mortar, with a little freestone employed in the jambs of the west windows. There is a well located in the central courtyard. During the 17th century the upper-storey rooms were reputedly decorated and the ceilings embellished with painted biblical scenes and texts. (Free admission. Open all times.)

12. EARL'S PALACE, KIRKWALL [450108]
Palace of Patrick Stewart, Earl of Orkney (1600), S.D.D.

Set immediately behind the Bishop's Palace and

opposite the cathedral, in its own tree planted grounds. It has been described as 'the most accomplished piece of Renaissance architecture in Scotland', although much of it is unfortunately now ruinous. It was built round three sides of a square with money and labour extracted from unwilling subjects, and 'in its combination of strength and elegance the residence of Earl Patrick Stewart was equally well adapted for war and wassail, for purposes of outrage and scenes of revel... it possessed from the first all the features of a robber's stronghold though adorned with the elegancies of a palace'. Whatever else Patrick Stewart can be accused of, bad taste may not be added to it. The principal features are a great hall and two smaller apartments on the first floor, with a series of cellars set below. There is much carved detail and adornment throughout, of both French and Elizabethan influence. Equally worthy of attention are the oriel and bay windows, and a fine lintelled fireplace. Less decorative, but equally significant, are the gun-loops in the sw facade. (Guide in attendance. Descriptive leaflet available. Entrance fee. *Standard Hours.*)

13. EYNHALLOW [359289]
Small island and site of ruined Norse and possibly Celtic churches (7th and 12th centuries), S.D.D.
Lying between Mainland and Rousay, and surrounded by fierce tide-races, Eynhallow rises to just over 100 ft. and barely exceeds 2/3 m. in any direction. The 12th century church overlooks Mainland, and consists of, besides the original features (the w & E gables of the nave, the porch and archways), a confused patchwork of later additional masonry, mostly 16th and 17th century in date. The existence of the chapel came to light in 1851, when the last four families on E. were evacuated due to persistent disease. Their home was unroofed, and only then was it realised that they had been living in a converted chapel. It seems likely that an even earlier Celtic chapel existed here. Reference is made in the *Orkneyinga Saga* to E. as *Eyin-Helga* (holy Isle) from which the foster-son of the famous chieftain, Kolbein Hruga, was kidnapped in 1155. His presence on E. could be explained by the existence of a monastery where he would have been schooled. The oldest elements of the group of buildings to the w of the church may constitute the remains of this. E. is hedged about with question marks, but the Norse name for it, its isolated character (so beloved of Celtic clergy), and the scale and dignity of the existing chapel (50ft. long and comprising chancel, nave and w porch) all point to an ancient and hallowed tradition here. (Free admission. Open all times.) Access by local boat-hire (see *The Islands*).

14. GRAEMSHALL, MAINLAND (484020)
Private antique collection (Norwood Collection)
On view to the public in the historic country house of G., 1m. E of St Mary's in the parish of Holm. Some fine porcelain, pottery, lustreware, silver and other objects of interest. (Entrance fee. *Tel. Holm 217).*

15. GRAIN EARTH HOUSE, MAINLAND [443118]
Souterrain, S.D.D.
Located ¾m. w of Kirkwall in Hatston Industrial Estate (signposted). First discovered in 1827, it went virtually ignored, until 1857, when it was re-ex-

cavated by an antiquary who, unfortunately, left scant record of what he found. The earth-house is set below ground level, and takes the form of a small kidney-shaped apartment, 12ft. long x 6ft. wide, reached via a series of descending steps and a curving, gently down-sloping passage, 16ft. long x 2½ft. wide x 3ft. high. Both passage and chamber are lintelled, the 5½ft. high ceiling of the chamber in addition being supported by four free-standing pillars. The roof of the chamber lies 7ft. below ground-level, and large quantities of shells, ashes and animal bones were found above it: however, no relic has ever been discovered within it, either upon its discovery or since. Very claustrophobic. (Free admission. *Standard Hours.*)

16. GURNESS BROCH, MAINLAND [383268]
(1st century B.C./A.D.-12th century A.D.) S.D.D.
Located 1½m. from A966 in Evie, on the seaward side of Aiker Ness, overlooking Eynhallow Sound. The massive remains of the broch are surrounded by a confusing jumble of later, additional constructions and walls, and the whole is enclosed within a circular ditch. It was built to meet a defensive need in troubled and dangerous times, but in the more stable period which followed its occupants erected a series of domestic buildings around and within it, utilising it in this way for many centuries. A small iron foundry was discovered here, and remains of what were probably several Viking longhouses were dismantled and rebuilt a little way from the broch. The grave of a 9th century Norse woman was discovered on the seaward side of the entrance causeway: she had been buried lying on her back in a stone-lined pit, wearing at her breast two large, oval, matching bronze brooches and dressed in a finely woven, woollen fabric; a shell necklace had been placed around her neck, a wooden-handled knife at her left side, and a small iron sickle at her right side. Pictish remains have also been found: a bone knife-handle with *ogam* inscriptions and a stone crudely carved with Pictish symbols. Today the broch stands only to a height of 12ft., and is entered via a low tunnel, off which lead two small intra-mural cells and a passageway. This last feature was reponsible for the early collapse of the broch structure—as with Mid-howe—and was probably a design error. The interior of the broch was partitioned into living areas, and another storey with stairways leading to it was evidently constructed at a later date. A fresh-water well is located within the courtyard. (Small museum on site and guide-book available. Entrance fee. *Standard Hours.*)

17. HEAD OF WORK, MAINLAND [483138]
Horned cairn
Situated 2½m. NE of Kirkwall, on the highest point of Head of Work. The 150ft. long and 50ft. wide turf covered mound is, to date, unexcavated. At either end of the tumulus are projecting 'horns', which form enclosures. Rare in Orkney.

18. HOLM OF PAPA WESTRAY [509518]
Late chambered-type cairn, S.D.D.
Located at the SE coast of this tiny uninhabited island, which it dominates from its highest point, above 60ft. high cliffs. The external dimensions measure 104ft. x 41ft., and within this mound is contained a chamber 67ft. long x 5ft. wide x 9ft. high. The entrance passage

is 18ft. long, but this is now blocked off, and access is obtained by way of the new concrete roof. The walls are 18ft. thick and contain twelve small mural cells; the chamber is compartmented in three sections by walls towards either end—each of these end sub-chambers contain three cells, and the main section has three cells along either side, one on each side being a double cell. This arrangement is unique amongst Orkney's cairns. Although only a small quantity of animal bones were found within, some inscriptions are carved into the walls, and these have been linked with representations of the human face such as those found at the chalk drum at Folkton, Yorkshire as well as similar Continental and Aegean motifs. (Free admission. Open all times.) Another cairn is located at the island's northern tip.

19. ITALIAN CHAPEL, LAMB HOLM [488006]

Near St Mary's, on the tiny island of Lamb Holm—which is connected to Mainland by the first of the Churchill Barriers—is a unique memorial to Orkney's inhabitation by 550 Italian prisoners-of-war in the 1940s. The chapel is all that remains of *Camp 60*, where they were interned, being a corrugated-iron nissen hut which was internally transformed into a beautiful little Catholic chapel. It is adorned with much freehand painting, and a few years ago was repainted and restored by the prisoner who originally executed the work.

20. KIRKWALL [450110]

Capital town of the Orkney Islands (pop. 4,800)

Kirkwall has been the commercial and administrative centre of these Islands since the 11th century at least, and there is evidence to suggest it was of importance long before that. It was one of the earliest Norse towns, and was formerly called *Kirkjuvagr* (Church-Bay) after the church built here by Earl Rognvald Bruisison around 1040 in memory of his friend, King Olaf Haraldsson—later the patron saint of Norway. (All that remains of this is a doorway in St Olaf's Wynd.) The Norse influence is still very evident in this inviting little town (which could quite truthfully be called a city, since it boats a cathedral), especially in the crow-stepped, gable-ended houses which encroach upon Bridge Street, Broad Street and Albert Street—which together formed the basis of the old town. The British visitor cannot fail to be impressed with the foreign flavour of the narrow, twisting, flagstone-paved streets and the evocative business names which adorn them—e.g. Flett, Rendall, Kirkness. In the old town there are few pavements; motorists and pedestrians happily co-exist on equal terms without benefit of modern traffic control systems—to the visiting city-dweller the absence of traffic lights, yellow lines, etc. will surely

come as a pleasant surprise—and weave, side-step and navigate their separate courses with a patience and ease bred of long practice. Shopping in Kirkwall still has an old-world charm about it for the most part, with friendly and personal service from family-run businesses stocking a wide (and sometimes remarkable!) range of goods. Knitwear, especially, is widely sold and represents good value. (Market-day—Monday; Early-closing—Wednesday.) St Magnus Cathedral has dominated Kirkwall since the 12th century, and with the Bishop's Palace and Earl's Palace (q.v.) formed the spiritual and temporal heart of the town and, indeed, Orkney itself. They lie close together in a vicinity known as the Laverock. The town formerly was possessed of a late-14th century castle, which was built by Lord Henry Sinclair, Earl of Orkney: Earl George of Caithness was driven to write while besieging it in 1614— 'I protest to God the house has never been biggit (built) without the consent of the devil, for it is one of the strongest holds in Britain—without fellow.' Unfortunately all that remains today is a weathered heraldic stone set into the s gable of a building at the e end of Castle Street. A charming 16th century building opposite the Cathedral—known as Tankerness House (q.v.)—has been converted into an interesting little folk-museum, and is well worth a visit. Amongst the other facilities which Kirkwall enjoys is a public library in Laing Street which claims to be the longest established in Britain (1683): temporary tickets are available, and for anyone interested in Orcadian or Norse subject matter, the Orkney Room is a must. Kirkwall was created a Royal Burgh in 1486 by King James III of Scotland, who also presented St Magnus Cathedral to its inhabitants. The original town followed the shoreline of the Peerie Sea—Kirkwall's harbour until the 19th century, when it was cut off to shipping, and since then largely infilled and built on. A rewarding view of the town and the North Isles can be had from the summit of *Wideford Hill* (741ft.), 2m.w of Kirkwall.

Airport 3½m. - Finstown 7m. - Maeshowe 9½m. - Ring of Brogar 11½m. - Stromness 15m. - Dounby 14m. - Skara Brae 17m. - Birsay 20m. - St Mary's 6½m. - St Margaret's Hope 14m.

21. KNAP OF HOWAR, PAPA WESTRAY [483519]

Neolithic dwellings (3500-3100 B.C.), S.D.D.

On the west coast of the island, overlooking the sea, stand the remains of two semi-detached dwellings of roughly oblong plan, resembling in some respects the secondary structures at the Broch of Gurness. The groundplan of the two huts is similar—both are crimped near the middle in figure-of-eight fashion and internally partitioned with projecting flagstones. They measure respectively 32ft. x 16ft. and 26ft. x 11ft.; both stand today to a maximum height of 5½ft. The first estimate of their age (in the 1930s) was based on discoveries of saddle and rotary querns, and fixed them in the Iron Age. In 1973 they were excavated again, this time by Dr Anna Ritchie; on this occasion radiocarbon datings of food refuse established these buildings as probably the oldest standing stone houses in NW Europe and the best preserved neolithic stone houses in Britain. Domestic refuse discovered beneath the foundations of the huts indicated that the site was in use prior to their construction. Flint, stone and bone artifacts dredged from the surrounding midden included a polished stone axe-head, whalebone mallets and a whalebone spatula. Animal bones identified numbered those of sheep, cattle, pigs and deer, besides limpet, whelk, oyster, scallop and razor-fish shells in large quantities. The larger building was apparently the main dwelling-house, and was divided by a partition of upright flagstones and two vertical timbers—which also acted as roof supports. The outer roomwas semi-paved, and contained a stone bench along one wall. The earth-floored inner room functioned as kitchen and workshop, and contained an open hearth and two stone querns: bedding grooves for wooden benches are still visible along each of the side walls, and a mural stone cupboard in the N wall. The other, smaller hut was built slightly later and was probably utilised as extra working space and storage: it was partitioned into three small rooms, and contained stone cupboards and compartments, two hearths—the earlier one is still visible — and a stone workbench. (Free admission. Open all times.)

22. KNOWE OF LAIRSO, ROUSAY [398279]
Horned cairn (3rd or 4th millennium B.C.)
Situated 400yds. E of Hullion near *B9064*. The 180ft. long mound has been much despoiled by farming operations, and contains a 17ft. long chamber, subdivided into three compartments by flagstone partitions down either side. It reaches 13½ft. in height. There is evidence of later intrusive building and alterations (circa 2400B·C·). Little was found inside apart from two small fragments of round-bottomed pottery and a small stone axe.

23. KNOWE OF SMIRRUS, MAINLAND [291215]
Bronze Age tumulus of large dimensions (2nd millennium B.C.)
Located ½m. N of Dounby and 400yds from *A986*. The mound measures 100ft. in diameter and attains 6ft. in height. It has been much disturbed, but the remains of what appears to be a cist can be detected amongst the ruins.

24. KNOWES OF TROTTY, MAINLAND [341175]
Bronze Age tumuli (2nd millennium B.C.)
Situated behind Netherhouse, between Midhouse and Winksetter (q.v.). There are a total of eleven mounds ranged along the lower slopes of Ward of Redland. Most have been disturbed. Three lie close together near the farm, and the largest of these consists of a 'platform', 80ft. x 93ft. x 3ft. high, upon which is heaped an oval tumulus, 61ft. x 55ft., to a height of 9ft. When this was opened in 1858 it was found to contain four gold 'sun-discs', amber beads and cremated bones.

25. KNOWE OF YARSO [404281]
Stalled cairn (early 3rd millennium B.C.), S.D.D.
Located 550yds. from *B9064*, opposite Tratland. It is of double-walled construction with a decorative outer wall similar to Midhowe Cairn. The mound measures 50ft. x 25ft., and contains a chamber 24ft. long x 5ft.

wide which is subdivided into a series of three stalled compartments. It is approached by a 13ft long entrance passage. The remains of at least twenty-nine individuals were discovered here (amongst these were fifteen skulls found placed in a row along one wall, facing inwards), as were the bones of thirty-six red deer, some sheep and a dog. Although 'longhead' neolithic skulls were identified, and radiocarbon datings of animal bones placed them around 2900 B·C·, fragments of a beaker and a food-vessel synonymous with the Bronze Age were discovered here too. (Free admission. Open all times.)

26. MAESHOWE, MAINLAND [318128]
Chambered cairn (circa 2750 B.C.), S.D.D.

Situated opposite Tormiston Mill in Stenness, 400yds. from *A965*. This is rightly considered to be the most magnificent example of its type in Western Europe, and one of the finest pieces of megalithic architecture in Britain. Such labour must have been involved in the quarrying and transportation of the stone required, and such care was exercised in its construction, that Maeshowe was, in all probability, the last resting place of a person or persons of singular veneration and importance. It consists of a mound 115ft. in diameter and 24ft. in height, which is entered via a passage 36ft. long, 4½ft. high and lined with enormous slabs—the largest weighs more than three tons. Within, this opens out into a corbelled, beehive-type chamber, 15ft. square and 12ft. high. Three mural cells are set into the walls to the left and right and facing the entrance, and these were once sealed with large masoned stones now lying on the floor. The masonry is so precise that in many places it is impossible to insert a knife-blade between the stones. In each corner are located rising buttresses, each constructed from a combination of large single slabs and smaller stones. Maeshowe is doubly unique in that it contains the second-largest collection of runic inscriptions and graffiti extant. These were carved by marauding Vikings in the 12th century whilst—as they claimed—plundering treasure and sheltering from storms. For these men to broach Maeshowe must have required a degree of courage, fraught as such an act was with the fear of preternatural revenge. Indeed, the runes inform us that some of the intruders lost their sanity. One rune boasts, 'Haakon single-handed bore treasures from this howe.' A second declares, 'Crusaders opened this mound.', and yet another observes, 'Many a proud lady, low-stooping, has entered here.', perhaps referring to female remains found within. Several inscriptions are less than delicate in expression—even employing the odd runic four-lettered word! One carving depicts the widely reproduced 'Maeshowe Dragon'. Preserved from the elements, these grafitti are as fresh as the day the axes gouged them out, and remind us that 'the writing on the wall' is no new phenomenon. The sun on mid-winter's day still probes down the entrance passage to shine briefly within the chamber—a small warmth for its former occupants on their long journey to eternity, and perhaps, a promise of renewal, the rebirth of all things. The whole is circumscribed by a low earthwork bank and ditch; radiocarbon dating of peat from the bottom of this placed its construction around 2750 B·C· There is an inspection light within, and the custodian lives at the farm beside Tormiston Mill. (Guidebook and postcards available. Entrance fee. *Standard Hours.*)

27. MIDHOUSE, MAINLAND [340182]
Old Orkney farmhouse
Located 2½m. s of Dounby and 1½m. along secondary road to E· This is a good example of an Orcadian longhouse with contiguous kiln, byre and barn. Flagstone furniture may be seen within, and it is in the custody of Kirkwall Museum, who have plans to transform it into a small folk-museum.

28. MIDHOWE BROCH, ROUSAY [371308] S.D.D.
Situated on the w coast of Rousay, just N of Eynhallow. The use of the singular is misleading, as there are three brochs within 500 yds. of one another—an unusual circumstance. This, the central and largest, is surrounded by sea on three sides, and defended on the fourth by two ditches and a thick stone wall. Between this and the broch lies a confused farrago of buildings, ruined by the ravages of time and sea. The base of M. is approximately 60ft. in diameter, with walls 12-15ft. thick which rise today to a height of 14ft. A cup and ring marked stone is incorporated into the NE wall; another is built into some later walling to the SE. The small entrance passage has little 'beehive' cells leading off either side; a narrow passage runs off from one of these and travels round within the circumference of the wall (as at Gurness)—an unusual feature, and probably responsible for the broch's partial collapse and subsequent buttressing. The first gallery is now ruinous and was entered by a doorway 6ft. above the inner floor level. A fresh-water spring (still flowing) supplied a stone water-tank located in the courtyard. Many secondary constructions within and without the broch are evident. The use of the singular is misleading—a small building to the left of the broch entrance contains a stone smelting hearth, and large amounts of iron slag were found here. However, no iron objects have been evinced—only a few bronze ornaments and bronze-working moulds. Large quantities of stone and bone utensils wre unearthed though, along with saddle and rotary querns, spinning whorls, bone weaving-combs, broken pottery and some Ro-

man ware (probably acquired by trading or raiding). (Free admission. Open all times.)

Nearby, ¾m. along the shore to s—The Wirk; a stone tower similar to Cubbie Roo's Castle which most likely dates from the 12th century, although additional walling is 16th-century.

29. MIDHOWE CAIRN, ROUSAY [372306]
Stalled cairn (3rd or 4th millennium B.C.), S.D.D.
This 'great ship of death', as it has been described, lies only a stone's throw from the broch of the same name. The mound measures 106ft. x 42ft., and encloses a 76ft. long inner chamber partitioned into twelve compartments by stone flags. The whole is protected by a 'hangar', within which run raised walkways and overhead lighting. The turf covering has been removed, revealing the 18ft. thick double-wall construction and decorative, 'herring-bone', outer stone courses. All the interments were found along the E side—seventeen adults, six adolescents and two children. Also identified were bones of sheep, ox, Orkney vole, birds and pig, a red deer antler and many limpet shells. Few artifacts came to light, but some shards of Onston-ware were discovered. A line of walling runs from the SE and NE corners of the mound, only to vanish—a connection with 'horned' cairns? Seven similar cairns have been found on Rousay. (Free admission. Open all times.)

While at M. on a fine day a walk to the summit of nearby Ward Hill is rewarded with magnificent views.

30. NOLTLAND CASTLE, WESTRAY [429488] (15th century) S.D.D.
Located ½m. w of Pierowall. This formidable stronghold (more properly known as *Notland*), bristling with gun-loops and built on a Z-plan, was the work of Thomas de Tulloch, Bishop of Orkney and Governor of the Earldom under Eric of Denmark. It was begun in 1422 and never completed. The castle's last episcopal owner was Bishop Adam Bothwell, who made it over to Sir Gilbert Balfour, his brother-in-law—then Master of Mary Queen of Scots Household, Sheriff of Orkney and Captain of Kirkwall Castle, and to whom Notland is often wrongly attributed. (He was involved in the murders of Cardinal Beaton and Darnley, and died for plotting against the King of Sweden in 1576.) Notland was prepared to shelter Mary when she escaped from Lochleven Castle, although this never transpired. The notorious Earl Patrick Stewart besieged it successfully; and later it sheltered the surviving officers of Montrose's defeated army. A fine vista is afforded by the battlements. (Free admission. Descriptive leaflet available. *Standard Hours.*)

31. NORTH GAULTON CASTLE, MAINLAND [216134]
Rock sea-stack
This stands just off the cliff-lined coast of sw Mainland, 2m. from Stromness. Turn off the *A967* road to Birsay at Quholmslie (below the Hill of Miffia) and follow the road to Mousland Farm. From here one travels WNW for 1m. across open moor. 'The Old Man of Hoy's younger brother' is perhaps not so high as its consanguine contemporary, but its slender 170ft. are more aesthetically pleasing. Another fine sea-stack, *Yesnaby Castle*, is located 2m. farther N.
(Please note the comments appended to the next description.)

TOP LEFT Dundas Street, Stromness circa. 1900. TOP RIGHT Bridge Street, Kirkwall circa. 1900. BOTTOM Albert Street, Kirkwall circa 1900. These scenes are little changed today: *Kirkwall Library.*

North Gaulton Castle, West Mainland—one of several impressive sea-stacks around Orkney's coasts, the result of gradual erosion and final collapse of the original, intervening cliff structure.

32. OLD MAN OF HOY [176008]
Rock sea-stack

Located on the spectacular NW coast of Hoy, 2 m. NW of Rackwick. Often described as 'Orkney's oldest inhabitant', and certainly one of its most famous, this is in fact the highest sea-stack in Britain, standing, as it does, 450 ft. above sea-level. Its fame partly derives from the successful televised climbing attempt made on it in 1967, although it was a first conquered in 1966 (see *Recreations & Amenities*—Rock Climbing).

Some say it is best seen from sea, some from landward, but in any event it should be seen if possible. The 'Old Man' is in reality only about 300 years old—in terms of its formation—and a mere stripling in geological reckoning. The precipitous cliffs which run from Rackwick (itself a hauntingly beautiful, almost-now-deserted village) to the Old Man, and on to the highest vertical cliffs in Britain at St John's Head, form one of the finest cliff walks in the country.

N.B. The reader will hardly need reminding that cliffs are potentially dangerous, and should be treated with respect. Failure to fully appreciate this has resulted in not a few fatal accidents in Orkney. Please exercise caution at all times, especially in windy conditions, when cliffs should preferably be avoided altogether.

33. ONSTON CAIRN, MAINLAND [283117]
Stalled cairn, S.D.D.

Situated near the tip of a low-lying spit of land beside Bridge of Waithe, 400yds. from road. Circular in plan, with a diameter of 45ft. or so, the outward appearance of the mound has been restored to resemble its original contours—it is clad in a protective concrete dome. The entrance passage is 19½ft. long, and opens on a chamber 21ft. in length. This is partitioned into five compartments by flagstones down either side, and, set into the wall of the central compartment, contains in addition a small beehive-shaped cell (in which were found two crouched skeletons), suggesting an inter-reaction between the stalled and chambered tomb builders. It was first excavated in 1884, and gave up the largest single find of neolithic pottery in Scotland—twenty-two vessels in all—and the term *Onston-ware* or *Unstan-ware* (as this monument is sometimes referred to) is now generic for its type. The collection is on display in the National Museum of Antiquities, Edinburgh. Many burnt and unburnt human and animal bones were also found here, as were four leaf-shaped flint arrowheads and a flint knife. There are some runic inscriptions incised on a stone opposite the entrance. (Free admission. *Standard Hours.*)

34. ORPHIIR ROUND CHURCH, MAINLAND [334044]
Ruined Norse church & settlement (12th century), S.D.D.

Set just back from Orphir Bay, ½m. from *A964*. All that stands today of this—probably the oldest remains of ecclesiastical worship extant in Orkney—is part of the apse and circular nave. It was modelled on the Church of the Holy Sepulchre in Jerusalem, and was built by Earl Haakon around 1120, after his pilgrimage to the Holy Land in atonement for the murder of Earl Magnus. Most of the church was de-molished in the 18th century to make way for a new church; this has more recently been demolished also—a condign fate. The nave was 20ft. in diameter and 15ft. high, and it was illuminated by a skylight. Similar structures are to be found in Prague. It was formerly known as Girth House, a name which derives from the old Norse word *grid*—i.e. peace or sanctuary. Nearby foundations once formed the basis of a Norse settle-ment, and this, together with a drinking-hall (probably the site of the present farmhouse), was the seat or *Bu* of Earl Paul, Haakon's son. (Free admission. Open all times.)

35. QUOYNESS CAIRN, SANDAY [677378]
Chambered cairn (early 3rd millennium B.C.), S.D.D.

Located at the SE coast of the Els Ness peninsula. This tomb bears a resemblance to Wideford Hill cairn. Entrance is gained via the roof—the original 25ft. long entrance passage being blocked off. The rectangular inner chamber measures 12½ft. x 5½ft. in area and has converging walls; off this lead six small intra-mural cells. Many human and animal remains were found throughout, including those of at least ten adults and five children in a cist within the main chamber, but of greater significance, a curious three-pointed imple-ment or ornament and a bone pin similar in their design to finds at Skara Brae, thereby dating Quoyness from the same period. In addition, radiocarbon analysis of human bones found here placed them around 2900 B·C· (Free admission. *Standard Hours.*)

36. RENNIBISTER EARTH HOUSE, MAINLAND [397127]
Souterrain, S.D.D.

Situated 300yds. from Kirkwall—Finstown road, at SE corner of Bay of Firth. The existence of R. first came to light in 1926, when a threshing machine caused its roof to collapse. The underground chamber is of hexagonal, 'beehive' construction, 11ft. x 9ft. x 5ft. high. The corbelled roof is supported by four stone pillars, and five small recesses are set into the walls. The original 12ft. long entrance passage is now blocked, and access is gained via the roof. When excavated, the entrance was clogged with black earth and shells: more curious, however, were the many dis-articulated human bones and skulls found within, particularly four skulls placed orderly alongside the base of one pillar. Altogether, the remains of six adults and twelve young people were identified. However, it is improbable that R. was conceived as a tomb, and evident that the bones were originally interred else-where. (Free admission. Open all times.)

37. RING OF BROGAR, MAINLAND [294134]
Standing stone circle, S.D.D.

Simultaneously the most widely known and most cryptic of Orkney's many monuments, this ranks as one of the finest stone circles in Britain. It is set in a splendid isolation of moorland between the lochs of Stenness and Harray and describes a circle some 115yds. in diameter. Sixty menhirs once stood here: now only twenty-seven are still erect; four more lie collapsed and the bases of another nine are visible. The tallest attains 15½ft. in height. The original layout of the circle was conceived and executed with a high degree of precision, and, it is believed, employed a standard unit of measurement known as the Megalithic yard—2.722 ft. (This unit is still in debate, but, assuming its veracity, would have represented here a degree of accuracy in construction approaching one part in two thousand!) The 340ft. diameter of the circle equates to 125 M yards or 50 M rods (1 M rod = 2.5 M yards). The stones were set six degrees apart, beginning at geographical north. One broken upright in the N sector is inscribed with some undeciphered Norse tree-runes. The circle is surrounded by a rock-cut ditch—originally up to 10ft. deep and 30ft. wide—and is bridged by causeways in the NW and SE sectors (a feature which probably dates Brogar's construction later than the Stenness henge with its single causeway). The interior of the circle has to date never been excavated.

The vicinity of Brogar resembles an archaeological pot-pourri: A little way to the E of the circle stands a lone menhir known as the *Comet Stone;* along with the stumps of two other stones it surmounts a low, circular, earthen platform 43ft. in diameter. A mound rises just outwith the S bank of the henge ditch, and another, known as Salt Knowe, some 100yds. to the SW: neither has been properly excavated, although the latter is known to contain a cist. A number of small tumuli to the SE are similarly undocumented. Of two bigger mounds by the shore of Loch Harray, the most northern of them, known as *Plumcake Barrow*, was excavated last century and found to contain two cists; these gave up a steatite cinerary urn and a pottery vessel, both containing cremated bones.

It has been postulated that the Ring of Brogar, together with its satellite monuments, formed a lunar observatory accurate to one arc minute ($\frac{1}{60}°$), and that the period when this function could have been viable lay between 1660 B C and 1460 B C Although it seems probable that the henge pre-dates this, and the antiquity of the barrows and mounds remains to be established, nevertheless this intriguing theory cannot be dismissed altogether. (Free admission. Open all times.)

38. ST MAGNUS CATHEDRAL, KIRKWALL

This magnificent medieval building has dominated the lives of the people of Orkney for more than 800 years. A beginning was made to it in 1137 by Earl Rognvald Bruisison, who dedicated it to his martyred nephew, Magnus, after wrestling the earldom from Earl Paul. The first stage was completed and consecrated by 1154. The Durham School of masons is believed to be responsible for its design and construction, which continued for another 300 years. Its most prominent feature is undoubtedly the superb red and honey-coloured sandstone. The cathedral's existence brought many learned and influential pilgrims to these distant Islands down the centuries, contributing not a little to Orkney's economy and reputation as seat of learning. In 1486 it became the property of the people, when King James III of Scotland granted it along with a Royal Charter to the Burgh of Kirkwall. Cromwell's soldiers used the steeple as a fortress and prison, and turned the nave into a stable and barracks. It was much restored in the 19th and 20th centuries, and is now in excellent repair. The bones of St Magnus and St Rognvald are sealed inside caskets within the pillars which formerly flanked the high altar. A fine view of Kirkwall and the islands can be had from the tower, and an excellent guidebook is on sale within the cathedral.

39. ST MAGNUS CHURCH, EGILSAY [466304]

Norse chapel (12th century), S.D.D.

This impressive structure dominates the island, and lies ¼m. E of Skaill pier. Almost intact, though roofless, its most unusual feature is a 48ft. high round tower (which originally stood to 65ft.), in design undoubtedly of Irish influence. Large stones set on edge in the walls of the church add a distinctive and interesting effect, and bear a similarity to masonry at Noltland Castle. The arched doorways in the S and N walls are original, as are the opposing windows in the centre of the nave: the other lintelled windows in the S wall are later additions. A small chamber over the chancel was known as 'Grief House,' from the Norse term *grid,* or sanctuary, and access to this was originally via a timber gallery which ran round the nave at the same level. It is just possible that Earl Magnus spent his last night on earth here, before his murder by Earl Haakon on April 16th, 1115; more probably, the present building dates from 1135. (Free admission. Open all times.)

40. ST TREDWELL'S CHAPEL, PAPA WESTRAY [496509]

Ruined Norse chapel (12th century), S.D.D.
Located towards the SE of the island, on a small pit of land projecting into the loch of the same name. This diminutive ruin stands on a mound which overlays earlier structures, and is of uncertain date. It extends to 29ft. in length and 24ft. in breadth. St Tredwell, or Triduana, was a Pictish female saint associated with the cure of eye troubles, having reputedly sacrificed her own. Bishop John of Caithness is said to have had his sight restored after making pilgrimage to her resting place at Restalrig, Edinburgh in 1201. It is possible, indeed probable, that this was the site of an earlier Celtic chapel. A nearby wall is all that remains of a broch, and from this leads a narrow underground passage which may constitute part of an earth house. (Free admission. Open all times.)

41. SKAILL, MAINLAND [596088]

Celtic and Norse settlements (7th-11th century)
Located on the NE coast of Deerness peninsula at Brough of Deerness, 1m. N of Sandside. Approachable only by rock climb, this is typical of the isolated

sites chosen by the early Celtic *Papae*. Six separate periods of building are apparent here, spanning almost five centuries. In the *Orkneyinga Saga* it is mentioned as the *Hlaupandanes* where, in a great hall, Thorkel Fosterer, a good friend of Earl Thorfinn and a favourite of King Olaf of Norway, slew Earl Einar in 1020.

Deerness is rich in sandy bays and impressive cliffs. At Sandside can be seen an extraordinary natural phenomonen known as *The Gloup*: boat trips under this can be arranged at Skaill. A Covenanters' Memorial 1½m. E of the Brough remembers the running aground and sinking of the *Crown*, a ship deporting captured covenanters to Virginia after the Battle of Bothwell Brig in 1679...the chained prisoners were drowned.

42. SKARA BRAE, MAINLAND [231187]
Neolithic village (3100 - 2450 B.C.), S.D.D.

The most-visited of Orkney's ancient monuments has been described as 'the most perfect Stone Age village in Europe', and represents a unique record of neolithic Man's domestic existence, remarkably preserved in the sands which eventually overwhelmed it. Set in the magnificent sweep of Skaill Bay, West Mainland, ½m. from the B9065, this Stone Age 'Ideal Home exhibition' consists of a group of ten corbelled stone huts of roughly rectangular configuration, furnished with flagstone box-beds, storage 'sideboards', central hearths, and small flagstone lined water-tanks set into the earth floors (which were probably used for keeping shellfish alive, or for softening-up limpets in fresh water for use as fish-bait). The huts were inter-connected by low, covered passageways threading between them, and a remarkable drainage system underlies the whole complex. Also evident is an open, paved communal courtyard. Any feelings of kinship for the long-departed members of this community are somewhat dulled by the knowledge that their homes were buried in their own middens; however these venerable rubbish tips yielded much useful information.

Remains of cattle, sheep, red deer, wild boar, fish, birds' eggs, and shell-fish in large quantities—mostly limpets—were identified—bearing silent witness to the fact that the people of S.B. were farmers, hunters, fishermen and food-gatherers. Other discoveries included fragments of wooden objects, short lengths of rope, carved 'spined' stone balls, ritual mace-heads and wall etchings. The remains of two old women were

discovered beneath the walls of one of the huts... a possible foundation rite? No trace of weaving has been found, however—the occupants of S.B. almost certainly dressed in skins, and their homes were probably roofed in the same way. Nevertheless, they had apparently acquired the art of making coarse pottery and cultivating crops—principally barley. No evidence of trading or metalworking has ever been found, and it seems likely that S.B. was a self-sufficient community.

Apart from the obvious durability of its stone construction, S.B.'s remarkable state of preservation can be attributed to its sudden inundation by sand—an event which forced its inhabitants to beat a hasty retreat, testified to, perhaps, by necklace-beads found scattered within one of the hut doorways. The refugees re-occupied their half-buried village (three separate levels of tenancy are evident), but the implacable tide of sand finally prevailed—and closed over it.

So it remained, unsuspected, until 1850, when a violent storm exposed it again. In all probability S.B. was originally ½m. from the sea, which has been steadily eating into Skaill Bay for centuries. In fact, the village would surely be devoured by now, had not a protective sea-wall been built in 1924—the year the then Office of Works assumed responsibility and serious preservation and excavation began. At that point S.B. was held to date from no earlier than the Christian era. Following further consolidation of the fabric in 1928 & 9—overseen by Professor Childe—a dating based on pottery finds placed it around 500 B C· Since then, however, it has been firmly established by radiocarbon techniques that the construction of S.B. was contemporary with the cairn-building period.

(Small museum on site with guide in attendance. Descriptive booklet and postcards available. Entrance fee.*Standard Hours.*)

The remains of the *Broch of Borwick* are located 1½m. directly S from here.

43. STONES OF STENNESS, MAINLAND [307125]
Standing stone circle (early 3rd millennium B.C.), S.D.D.

Situated 200 yds. SE from Bridge of Brodgar, beside B9055. Originally twelve uprights stood here: today only four survive—of varying heights, the greatest of which exceeds 17ft.—and describe part of a circle which, if it were complete, would measure more than

A *Perspective View of the Standing* Stones *in the Parish of Stainhouse in Orkney.*

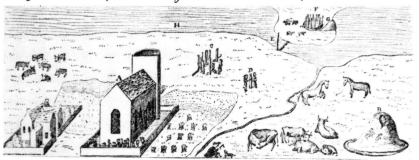

100ft. in diameter. An encircling, rock-cut ditch, 200ft. in diameter, can still be traced in places, and was formerly complemented by an outer raised earthwork; this was bridged by a single entrance-causeway in the N sector. In 1906 a spurious, dolmen-type construction was caused to be erected by misguided archaeological thought as 'restoration', although this has since been cast down by persons unknown. A setting of horizontally laid stones describing a square in the centre of the circle yielded up during excavations fragments of animal bones and grooved-ware pottery (as did the encircling ditch), suggesting feasting or sacrificial rites; but, of more importance, it established beyond doubt that this monument was contemporary with Skara Brae and the cairn builders.

Nearby, standing sentinel by the Bridge of Brodgar, can be found the massive menhir known as the *Watch Stone* — 18½ ft. in height, and the lone survivor of a group of three. Another, which stood a little to the E of the last named, was removed during the 19th century—the *Stone of Odin* (see *Superstitions & Customs*). Two smaller uprights only a yard apart and the remains of a low mound are located a short distance to the NW, beside the road. The strong impression of some form of processional way between the Stones of Stenness and the nearby Ring of Brogar is as difficult to avoid as it is attractive, although this is impossible to confirm. (Free admission. Open all times.)

44. STROMNESS, MAINLAND [253090]
Orkney's second town (pop. 1,700)

Tucked into the SW corner of Mainland, with its face to the sea and the rising sun, Stromness provides most of Orkney's visitors with their first taste of the Islands—and no bad one at that. As the Scrabster ferry glides gently past the *Holms*—the little tidal islands which enclose the harbour—the eye is greeted by serried ranks of stone houses and small jetties jostling for elbow-room beside the town's waterfront. Many visitors make straight for Kirkwall as soon as they disembark—which is rather a pity, for Stromness must surely be one of Britain's most picturesque towns. The old Norse name for S. was *Hamnavoe*, literally Haven-Bay, and it was this sheltered anchorage which was to become the town's *raison d'être* and greatest asset. The town one sees today, however, dates from the 17th and 18th centuries.

During this period the shipping which took the Northabout Route in preference to the English Channel found this a convenient staging point. Local enterprise was not slow to capitalise on the provisioning of visiting vessels and catering for their crews—and their appetites (up to forty 'inns' vied with each other at one stage!). Business thrived, and along the waterfront gable-ended buildings, nousts (slips) and quoys (piers) grew in profusion; more buildings were added piecemeal and spread up the slope behind. The main thoroughfare was little more than an alley pushing between this architectural Donnybrook Fair, in places only a yard wide and running the entire length of the town. Although this has been widened, the result today is a narrow, meandering, flagstone-paved street, 'uncoiling like a sailor's rope', and an adventure to walk down in more than one respect—it was conceived before the horseless carriage. A labyrinth of closes, alleys, vennels and steps vanishes enticingly seawards and mysteriously uphill, including—in this last-mentioned category—the notably and aptly named *Khyber Pass*. No modern planning department would have tolerated this happy anarchy, but perhaps we should be thankful that such a worthy and vigilant body did not exist 200 years ago....

Even today much of the town's economy is based on trading, and there is a wide range of shops. (Early-closing—Thursday; Market-day—Wednesday.) Local industries include boatbuilding, fishing and Orkney Fudge manufacture. A lifeboat and the Northern Lighthouse Board's supply ship *Pole Star* are also based here. The town's facilities include a new arts centre and gallery with its own permanent collection, a small museum, a public library (visitors tickets available), a swimming pool, an 18-hole golf course and a modern sports and social complex (bowls and tennis). In mid-July each year a deceptively titled 'Stromness Shopping Week' heralds seven days of entertainment, dances, concerts, shows, exhibitions and parades, culminating in a barbecue and fireworks display. Brinkie's Brae, the hill behind the town, affords an excellent vista, and the westward coastal path leading to the old graveyard constitutes a fine walk with good views of Hoy. There are regular buses to Kirkwall and elsewhere, and both cars and bicycles may be hired here. (See also *The Sea*.)

In 1758 the town was recognised as a Free Burgh, thanks to the efforts of Alexander Graham, who loosed S. from the yoke of Kirkwall and its stranglehold powers of taxation. This eventually paved the way for the breaking of similar monopolies throughout Scotland.

Maeshowe 5½m. - Ring of Brogar 6¼m. - Finstown 8m. - Kirkwall 15m. - Skara Brae 7½m. - Dounby 9½m. - Birsay 14m.

45. TANKERNESS HOUSE, KIRKWALL [448109]
Folk museum and typical merchant's town house (16th century)

Facing St Magnus Cathedral, this fine example of solid Scottish architecture was built by Gilbert Filzie, archdeacon to the cathedral prior to the Reformation. One of Orkney's oldest landed families, the Baikies of Tankerness, owned it for more than three centuries. Since 1968, however, it has served as a museum, and currently houses an absorbing collection of Orcadian historic and domestic relics, besides mounting regular exhibitions. Entrance is free, although all contributions will be gratefully received. The peaceful and sheltered gardens behind the house provide an excellent retreat from the bustle of Kirkwall.

46. TAVERSOE TUICK, ROUSAY [426276]
Double, stalled cairn, S.D.D.
Located just ½m. w of Brinyan pier, beside the road.

This is a rare example of a two-storeyed tomb, and, after Maeshowe, perhaps Orkney's most noteworthy cairn—as regards design at least. The upper chamber, which rests on the roof of the lower, is 16ft. long, much ruined and entered from the N. The lower is better preserved, measures 12ft. x 5ft. x 5ft. high, contains four stalled cells and is entered by a 19ft. long passage from the S. Both chambers are subterranean in nature, with foundations dug through clay into rock. The whole is enclosed within a tumulus 30ft. in diameter. The lower chamber gave up unburnt human bones and fragments of Onston-type pottery; in the passage burnt bones and a granite hammer-head were found.

An unusual circumstance here was the discovery of a small underground chamber some 20ft. from the entrance to the lower tomb. Oval in shape, and only 5ft. x 4ft. x 3ft. high, it is carefully constructed, roofed with flagstones and partitioned by four upright stone slabs radiating inward from the walls; three neolithic pots were found within. (Free admission. Open all times.)

Another two-storeyed tomb was discovered at Huntersquoy, Eday.

47. TORMISTON MILL, MAINLAND [319125]
Restored water-mill (1844)
Situated beside the *A965*, directly opposite Maeshowe. A former meal-grinding mill, it has since been converted into a craftshop and licensed restaurant. The original workings, however, may still be seen.

48. WESTNESS, ROUSAY [383290]
Norse settlement (9th - 12th century)
Overlooking Eynhallow, beside the *B9064*. A treasure laden 9th century grave was excavated here, and points to the importance of this site in early Norse settlement. Further discoveries of 10th century Viking pagan graves support this view. A series of buildings which also came to light here are believed to have been the abode of Sigurd of Westness, an influential Norseman in the 12th century. In 1136 Earl Paul was kidnapped at Westness by the legendary Sweyn Asliefson.

49. WESTRAY CHURCHES [455432 & 440488]
Norse churches (12th and 13th century), S.D.D.
The first of these, **Westside Church,**lies near the *Point of the Scurroes,* 3½m. s of Pierowall. It is dedicated to the Holy Cross, dates from the 12th century and, although roofless, remains largely intact. The chancel entrance and arch still stand, as do an original door and window in the nave; this last was extended from its original 19ft. to a length of 47ft. at a later date.

The other chapel, **St Mary's,** is set towards the N of Pierowall Bay, and was built during the 13th century. Much reconstructed at later periods, it consists of nave—widened during the 17th century—and chancel. Two interesting gravestones can be inspected at the E end of the church—probably the previous location of the now vanished chapel in which Earl Rognvald went

to service upon his arrival in Orkney in 1136. (Free admission. Open all times.)

50. WIDEFORD HILL CAIRN, MAINLAND [409122]
Early chambered cairn , S.D.D.
Located 2½m. w of Kirkwall, ½m. from *A965* below Wideford Hill. Although similar to Maeshowe in many respects, its construction is on a much less grandiose scale. The earth covering has been removed to reveal that this is of a three-tiered type, with external diameters of 42ft., 34ft. and 25ft. respectively, and foundations dug into the hillside. The beehive-shaped inner chamber, 10½ft. x 4½ft. and rising to 8ft., contains three mural cells; a 17½ft. long entrance passage runs into it from the w. Looters long ago plundered this cairn, and no human remains have been subsequently found here. However, bones of horse, cow, sheep and deer were identified. Entrance is now gained via a roof-hatch. (Free admission. Open all times.)

51. WINKSETTER, MAINLAND [341164]
Early Norse dwelling
Located below Burrien Hill, ¾m. from *A986* in Harray. This could be the oldest standing Norse building in Orkney. Now doing service as a byre, it takes the form of a long, low structure built down a slight slope, and is consequently stepped. The living quarters lay behind and were entered via the original byre—which was an integral part of the building—and consisted of a larger and a smaller room, flagstone paved throughout. The first room has since been subdivided. It contains a stone corner-shelf, where a mortar and pestle for corn-grinding were kept, and an intra-mural hen roost; in the next section may be seen intra-mural stone cupboards and a goose-nest. This was the fire-room, with a free-standing fireback set in it. To the rear of this was the living-room, now half its original length; more store cupboards and an ale-recess are visible here. Another byre formerly ran parallel to this structure, separated by a narrow alley-way which was blocked at one end against the wind. Other buildings have since vanished. Although Winksetter's origins are still open to speculation it is almost certainly Norse: its thick walls, stepped construction and its windows are characteristic of similar buildings in Ireland know to be so. One school of thought suggests that it might have been a Norse hunting lodge.

52. WYRE CHAPEL [443264]
Ruined Norse chapel (12th century), S.D.D.
Situated within a stone's throw of *Cubbie Roo's Castle* (q.v.), this pint-sized Romanesque chapel was most probably likewise built by Kolbein Hruga. It consists of a nave (19ft. x 13ft.) and chancel (8ft. x 7ft.). The entrance arch, doorway and chancel arch are original, but the s wall windows have been altered. It never attained the status of parish church. (Free admission. Open all times.)

N.B. The prehistoric dating used throughout this book is of the calibrated radiocarbon type—a discrepancy between empiric radiocarbon dating and growth-ring dating of Californian bristle-cone pine was discovered some years ago, and, based on this, it is now generally held that a corrected or calibrated figure provides a true date. (e.g. Skara Brae: radiocarbon dates—2500/2000 B.C.; calibrated dates—3100/2450 B.C.)

The Islands

O F THE TWENTY-TWO secondary islands given here, only four are totally uninhabited; nearly all have something to offer the visitor, however. Some are more accessible than others—a double-edged advantage/disadvantage, depending on one's point of view. Since **Burray** and **South Ronaldsay** are no longer separate island entities in the true sense of the word (connected, as they are, to Mainland by those wartime structures, now causeways, the Churchill Barriers) they tend to be amongst the most frequented.

Although the more remote islands are devoid of a sophisticated tourist industry, they are not without facilities—nine-hole golf courses on **Westray** and **Sanday**, and, in many instances, boat, car and bicycle hire. There are many fine beaches and sheltered bays (particularly **Sanday**), numerous cliffs and bird colonies, and enough historic sites to keep the most avid antiquary busy for the rest of his allotted span! Life continues at a steady, unhurried pace, as it has done for centuries, and the visitor is received as an honoured guest—only the sheep are fleeced.... (Hotels are listed, but most islands offer bed and breakfast and self-catering facilities—details from Orkney Islands Tourist Organisation.)

The Orkney Islands Shipping Co. operates services most days to **Eday, Stronsay, Sanday, Papa Westray,** and**Westray,** and less frequently to **Rousay, Egilsay, Wyre, North Ronaldsay, Shapinsay, Flotta, Graemsay** and **Hoy** *(Lyness and Longhope).*

Mr Magnus Flaws operates a twice-daily service from Tingwall Pier (6m. N of Finstown) to **Rousay** and **Wyre,** and less frequently to **Egilsay.** (Also charter-hire to **Eynhallow, Gairsay,** etc.)

A regular daily ferry plies between Stromness and **Hoy** *(Linksness),* and a private Kirkwall-**Shapinsay** service is in operation.

Regular inter-island flights are operated by Loganair to and from **Eday, Flotta, Hoy, North Ronaldsay, Papa Westray, Sanday, Stronsay, Westray** and Kirkwall. (Charters available.)

The above information is intended only as a guide: the intending traveller should check all details before setting out. Comprehensive timetables are published weekly in *The Orcadian,* and may also be obtained from the respective operators. (For details of transport operators see *Useful Information*—q.v.)

AUSKERRY: Uninhabited, tiny island, 3m. S of Stronsay. Good bird migration watching point with some small seabird colonies. Standing stones, burnt mounds and a ruined chapel may be seen. Unmanned lighthouse located at S end of island.

BARREL OF BUTTER: Uninhabited rock in middle of Scapa Flow. The curious name derived from the form of payment made in medieval times by the inhabitants of Orphir to their lord for the right to kill seals here.

BURRAY, pop. *under 300:* Lies between Mainland and S. Ronaldsay and joined to each by the Churchill Barriers. Extensively farmed island with a beautiful sandy bay on E coast. *Echna Loch* much frequented by wintering wildfowl. A group of three brochs on N coast gave B. its name, which literally means 'fortress-island'. Formerly the property of Earl Patrick Stewart, whose residence stands on the E coast. At the *Wha Taing*—near the adjacent holm of *Hunda* (which is joined to B. by a reef)—copper was once mined. The island was formerly a herring fishing base—net warehouses can still be seen at the pierheads; and the small village of Burray contains a boatbuilding yard owned by the same family for five generations. [Pop. (1881) 685.]

CAVA: Uninhabited island, 1 m. long, between Flotta and Graemsay. Gow, the pirate, ran aground on the *Calf of Cava*, where an unmanned lighthouse is now located. [Pop. (1861) *29.*]

COPINSAY: Uninhabited (apart from lighthouse). Minute attractive island, 2 m. s of Deerness, Mainland. It rises to a height of 150ft. Some of the most important seabird cliffs in Orkney, with many large colonies—especially Guillemot and Kittiwake—located here. Now designated a bird sanctuary, dedicated to the memory of the famous ornithologist, the late James Fisher. Bronze Age cist on nearby *Black Holm.*

EDAY, pop. (1974) *168:* One of the larger Northern Isles, of which it is central. There are some fine beaches and cliffs, many of the latter being inhabited by large seabird colonies—particularly *Red Head,* at N tip of island. *Mill Loch* is the haunt of Red Throated Divers. Along with Rousay, E. contains the greatest density of chambered cairns in Orkney. Traces of early Celtic settlement are also evident. The pirate, John Gow, was captured here in 1725: stains on the floor of *Carrick House* are attributed to his blood (see *The Sea*). The Earl of Carrick attempted to establish a Burgh of Carrick and a herring fishing industry here during the 19th century, but untimely death intervened before this was realised. A thriving trade in peat for Scottish distilleries existed here at that time. [Pop. (1851) *947.*]

EGILSAY, pop. *under 50:* Situated off E coast of Rousay. Flat, carrot-shaped island, 3 m. long and 111ft. high. It is dominated by 12th-century St Magnus Church, and was the scene of Earl Magnus's martyrdom in 1115. [Pop. (1831) *228.*]

EYNHALLOW: Uninhabited little island between Mainland and Rousay, surrounded by fierce tidal currents and shrouded in legend. It is of great historical interest as the possible site of an early Celtic community (q.v. *Historic Monuments &c.*). Breeding colonies of Fulmar and Black Guillemot. [Pop. (1841) *26.*]

FARA: Uninhabited island, 1¾ m. in length, situated between Hoy and Flotta. A possible candidate for oil-related development. [Pop. (1891) *76.*]

FLOTTA, pop. *160 (indigenous—see below):* This 3 m. wide island, which lies just off the E coast of Hoy, has lately assumed in Orkney an importance out of all proportion to its size. As if to underline this, the island, despite its low profile, is now conspicuous from much of Orkney: the phenomenon which attracts so much attention, known to many as the 'Flotta Flare,' is a huge flame of burning petroleum gas from Occidental's oil storage terminal here. Oil is piped from the *Piper* and *Claymore* oilfields in the North Sea to the seven huge storage tanks recently built on F., later to be shipped away for processing elsewhere. A workforce of several hundred men are permanently employed, and many live on site. (Intending visitors to the site must first obtain a security pass—not always granted.) [Pop. (1881) *425.*]

GAIRSAY: Thinly inhabited little island, 1¾ m. wide, between Shapinsay and Rousay. The 12th-century remains of Sweyn Asleifson's 60ft. long drinking-hall can be seen at *Langskaill.* This doughty old pirate—a contemporary of Earl Rognvald—lived here with eighty followers, and every spring after sowing was done a-Viking did go. He was eventually killed in Dublin. A fine view of the Islands is obtained from the 334ft. high summit of G. [Pop. (1821) *79.*]

HOY, pop. *550:* Second-largest of the Isles, and, unlike the others, almost mountainous in appearance. Extending to 12m. in length, it attains a height of 1,570ft. (*Ward Hill*). Some of the most spectacular cliffs in Britain plunge precipitously downwards from the island's desolate W coast—including *St John's Head,* at 1,140ft. the highest vertical cliff in the

country, located 5m. N of the **Old Man of Hoy.** This 'botanical treasure-house of Orkney', as H. has been dubbed, is the home of the Islands' only indigenous trees, besides some rare alpine flowers. There are many important seabird cliffs, including *The Berry* and *Too of the Head.* Red Throated Divers breed in the hill lochans; the moorlands shelter nesting Arctic Skuas and Great Skuas; and, for good measure, Manx Shearwaters and Peregrine Falcons thrive here. H. is also the home of the rare alpine hare—and not so rare midge, which breed in uncomfortably large numbers. The curious and interesting **Dwarfie Stone** may be seen near the road which leads to *Rackwick*—now an almost deserted village, set in a timeless, cliff-bound valley on the W coast. The pace of life in the little community of *Lyness* is no longer what it was either—naval camps were located here during two world wars. One of the island's two Martello towers is located a short distance SE of Lyness, and the other at *Hackness, South Walls.* Defensive structures which were formerly armed with 24-pounder cannons, they were built, not against the threat of Napoleon and French invasion, as most were, but as a deterrent to harassment of Britain's Baltic trade by the United States navy and American privateers. They were renovated in 1866, and utilised during World War I. The latter tower is in the care of the Department of the Environment, and restoration work is being carried out. [Pop. (1851) *1,555.*] *Longhope Hotel,* tel. Longhope 276; *Stroma Bank Hotel,* tel. Longhope 338. (No shop on North Hoy—take provisions with you.)

NORTH RONALDSAY, pop. (1974) *140:* Orkney's most northerly and easterly isle. Only 3m. long, it is low-lying and fertile, and circumscribed by a high stone dyke, outwith which live its famous seaweed-eating sheep—their mutton has a unique flavour! Seals are much in evidence here, as is birdlife—this is an ideal migration watching site. There are beaches to the E and s· and several archaeological sites, including the *Broch of Burrian*, where an ox-bone inscribed with Pictish symbols and a stone bearing the Celtic *Cross of Burrian* were found; the latter now much reproduced as jewellery. The island's most prominent feature is the lighthouse at its N end, first lit in 1854 and the highest land-based one in Britain: now disused, Orkney's first lighthouse (1789) can also be seen here. [Pop. (1881) *547.*]

PAPA WESTRAY: One of the most northerly islands, 4m. long, 1m. wide and low lying. The important role it played in both neolithic and Norse settlement can be ascribed to its soil, which is unusually fertile; this continues to be extensively cultivated today. *North Hill*, the rough moorland towards the north, is rich in flora and fauna, and is the haunt of important colonies of Arctic Tern, Arctic Skuas and Great Skuas (recently designated a nature reserve). *Fowl Craig* to the NE was the site of the last Great Auk colony in Orkney. *Loch of Tredwell* shelters many breeding birds and much waterfowl. The island boasts several historic sites, including what is probably the oldest neolithic dwelling in NW Europe, the **Knap of Howar** (see also **St Tredwell's Chapel** and **Holm of Papa Westray**). P.W. is mentioned in the *Guinness Book of Records*—the shortest scheduled flight in the world operates between here and Westray, a distance of 1½m. [Pop. (1861) *392.*]

ROUSAY, pop. (1974) *265:* This hilly island lies less than 1m. off NE Mainland, separated from it by the swift-flowing waters of *Eynhallow Sound.* The interior is virtually uninhabited, and the main road runs more or less round and parallel with the island's coast, the NW and SE extremities of which lie 6m. apart. It has been dubbed 'Egypt of the North,' a reference to the profusion of prehistoric monuments here—including the greatest density of chambered cairns in Orkney. *Blotchnie Fiold*, the highest hill (821ft.), affords a fine panoramic view of the Islands, and there are some excellent cliff-walks to the west and north. One of these cliffs, Hellia Spur, in the island's NW corner, is an important seabird colony. Outwith Mainland, some of Orkney's best trout fishing can be had from R.'s hilllochs and burns. Copper was once mined at *Westness,* the site of an early Norse settlement. In the farmyard here can be seen a small boat of old Norse designwhich two young Norwegians navigated to Orkney in best Viking tradition to fight for the Allies during World War II. R. suffered greatly in the 19th century at the hands of its then proprietor, General Borroughs, a man who preferred sheep to tenants. Today farming dominates R., although a crab-processing factory operates here too. The island is serviced by Orkney's first postbus. [Pop. (1841) *976.*] *Taversoe Hotel,* Frotoft, tel. R. 325.

SANDAY, pop. (1974) *598:* One of the largest of the Northern Isles. It extends to 13m. in length, is lowlying and widely farmed. As the name suggests, its most notable features are the number of fine beaches and miles of gold and silver sands. Every spring the dunes are thickly carpeted with wild-flowers, and

many species of birds build their nests amongst them. All round the island are good sea fishing waters, and a nine-hole golf course has opened recently. There are several archaeological sites, especially on the *Els Ness* and *Tres Ness* ayres in the SE, including **Quoyness Cairn.** Sanday Lighthouse is one of Britain's oldest: it

was badly needed—many boats came to grief on S.'s inconspicuous shores before it was built. The island's name is synonymous with knitting, and a knitter's co-operative flourishes here, as does a small electronics factory (q.v.—*Industry*). [Pop. (1881) *2,075.*] *Kettletoft Hotel,* tel. S 217.

SHAPINSAY, pop. (1974) *339:* This is a low island, less than 5m. wide, located only a long stone's throw from Mainland and just N of Kirkwall. Its soil is rich and fertile, and the island is well known for the quality of its cattle. There are several miles of sandy coast, especially to the W and N, and a fair scatter of minor archaeological sites, particularly brochs. There may have been a brief Roman presence on S.: the place-name *Grukalty* (or Grucula) is said to derive from Agricola, the Roman general who led an expedition to the Orkneys in A·D· 78. Baronial styled Balfour Castle was built in 1847 by Colonel David Balfour. He was a great agricultural improver who eventually caused an almost tenfold increase in S.'s arable acreage. [Pop. (1881) *974.*]

SOUTH RONALDSAY, pop. (1974) *1,002:* With the exception of Mainland, to which it is connected by the **Churchill Barriers,** this 8m. long island receives more visitors than any other. There are some fine sands in the vicinity of St Margaret's Hope, and interesting cliffs, geos and caves, mostly on the E coast. The little community of Herston—a former herring curing port—overlooks the sheltered sands of *Widewell Bay,* a boating and fishing mecca. The island's principal centre of population is *St. Margaret's Hope,* a fair sized hamlet which grew up around a busy 19th century herring-fishing station, long defunct.

It takes its name from the ill-fated Maid of Norway, who died here on 16th November 1290, aged seven, from the rigours of her wild passage from her native country. ('Hope' itself derives from *höp*—the head of a fjord.) Today, with a population of 250 or so, things are quieter here than formerly, and amongst the amenities available are two licensed hotels, a restaurant, tennis court, bowling green, information office and bank. The *Festival of the Horse* and *Boys' Ploughing Match* are annual and colourful events which take place in mid-August (see *Superstitions & Customs*). S.R. is not notably rich in archaeological sites. Just over 1m. w of S.M.'s H., however, the remains of a broch may be seen, and a cairn is located on the summit of *The Wart*, the evocatively named, low hill to the E of this. Many visitors to Orkney arrive by ferry from John O' Groats at *Burwick*, near S.R.'s southern tip, location of *St Mary's Church* and site of an anterior Celtic chapel; a little to the w are the remains of an earlier fort and settlement. [Pop. (1841) *2,580.*] *Bellevue Hotel,* tel. S.M.'s H. 383; *Murray Arms Hotel,* tel. S.M.'s H. 205.

STRONSAY, pop. (1974) *485:* Bar Auskerry, this is the most south-eastern of the Northern Isles. It is 7m. long, low-lying, fertile and extensively farmed. *White-hall,* the island's commercial centre, was formerly a herring-fishing boom town with up to 500 boats operating from it. Today its busy fishing community keeps a modern processing factory supplied with white fish, which is filletted and frozen for export to America. The island possesses many fine, sheltered bays and sandy beaches. An impressive gloup is located at *Vat of Kirbuster* in the SE, and the nearby *Brough* is a popular nesting place with Puffins. *Rothiesholm Head* in the sw is another good seabird cliff. The old well at *Kildinguie,* ¾m. s of Whitehall, was once highly regarded for the medicinal properties of its waters, which supposedly cure anything—with the exception of Black Death—when they are imbibed in conjunction with dulse from *Geo Odin*! Only a few years ago an elderly German lady with Parkinson's Disease made pilgrimage to it. A broch and a cairn are situated respectively at the E and w extremities of *Bay of Houseby* on the island's s coast. *Bay of Holland* in the sw witnessed the presence of 100 stranded whales in 1950. [Pop. (1871) *1,267.*] *Stronsay Hotel,* Whitehall, tel. S. 213.

SULE SKERRY: Uninhabited rock, apart from lighthouse, 37m. w of Brough Head, Mainland, less than ½m. long. It is probably better known as one of Britain's most remote lighthouses and weather stations than an island. However, it is densely populated with seals—several hundred of which were killed each year by Stromness folk—and houses the largest colony of Puffins in Orkney; it was also popularised in *The Ballad of Sule Skerry,* a tale of seal people.

WESTRAY, pop. (1974) *853:* Of all the outer islands, W has the best balance of upland and lowland. It is one of the larger Northern Isles, four pronged in configuration and 10m. long. There are some good sandy beaches—especially to the s—and the cliffs to the NW shelter the greatest density of breeding seabirds in the Islands, principally Guillemots, Auks and Kittiwakes. In fact, W is an ornithologist's delight with, besides cliff colonies, nesting duck, Snipe, Lapwing, Curlew, Corncrake and Oyster-Catchers. There is a nine-hole golf course near *Pierowall*--the small village formerly known as *Pirivaa*, the second most important Viking base in Orkney. A 13th-century Norse church

lies towards the N of the bay, and a 15th-century castle is located just w of the village (see **Westray Churches** and **Noltland Castle**). 2½m. farther w can be seen *Gentleman's Cave,* situated 1m. below *Noup Head:* it sheltered a group of Jacobites from English reprisal after the '45 rebellion. Previous to this a Spanish galleon was wrecked off W. at the time of the Armada; some physical traits of the island's inhabitants are said to have their origins in this event. More recently a crab-processing plant was established in Pierowall. An excellent panoramic view can be obtained from *Fitty Hill* (557ft.) in the sw. [Pop. (1881) *2,190.*] *Pierowall Hotel,* tel. W. 208.

WYRE: An attractive little island lying just off the s coast of Rousay. It extends to 2m. in length, and is named after its shape—i.e. *vigr,* or spearhead. There are beaches towards the N or s, and two interesting monuments—**Cubbie Roo's Castle** and **Wyre chapel** [Pop. (1841) 96.]

Recreations & Amenities

A NYONE WHO HAS experienced the rich social life typical of most rural communities will probably not be surprised to learn that a long winter's night in the Orkney Islands need not necessarily always be spent knitting Fair Isle sweaters or fashioning straw-backed chairs... betimes fetching a few more peats for the fire. Admirable pursuits though these be, Orkney has much more to offer. Whilst many indoor events are staged throughout the year, the summer months are enlivened with a broad range of *al fresco* activities. Details of these are published weekly in *The Orcadian* and in a broadsheet issued by the Orkney Tourist Organisation. In addition, Radio Orkney broadcast a 'What's On' feature every morning in their *Morning Magazine* (VHF only—93.7 MHz). There are many clubs and societies—even a War Games Society—and most of these welcome visitors. In fairness, however, it should be pointed out that North Ronaldsay has not, as yet, acquired a bingo hall or casino....

ARTS & CRAFTS: Privately arranged courses in basic spinning, weaving, painting, etc. are available during the summer—details from Orkney Tourist Organisation. In winter months many evening classes are held, covering a wide spectrum of activities. Art and craft materials are sold in Kirkwall and St Margaret's Hope.

BADMINTON: Court at Kirkwall Grammar School sports complex: check with Orkney Tourist Organisation regarding availability. Also featured as a regular winter activity in community halls.

BEACHCOMBING: Many of Orkney's shores are tailor-made for the purposes of this gentle pursuit/educational activity/idle amusement/uncertain profession. The regurgitated riches of the deep which one is liable to encounter are manifold—everything from dead wellies to deceased whales! The Northern Isles are a particularly good hunting-ground, with miles of sheltered bays and beaches (esp. *Sanday*).

BOAT TRIPS: These are numerous, and vary from 'trips round the bay' to excursions to Shetland and the Faroes. A round trip to the Northern Isles usually sets off every Monday and Friday from Kirkwall. Cruises to the Southern Isles sail from Stromness most Thursdays and Sundays (*summer only*). There are many more sailings—details locally or from Orkney Islands Tourist Organisation. Private charters available on most islands.

BOTANY: The rich variety of plant life on Hoy has already been referred to: besides rare alpines, it is graced with Orkney's only indigenous trees—rowan, hazel, aspen, sallow, etc. Orkney's sand dunes encourage Marram and Lyme grass, but the broad expanse of machair are carpeted with Eyebright and Gentianella during the month of June—watch out for the nests of Ringed Plover and Tern; some interesting maritime vegetation flourishes at *Waulkmill Bay* in Orphir; Sea-Arrow grass can be found in fresh-water marshes; a rare sea-sedge thrives under the radio mast on *Wideford Hill*; and not a few sheltered clifftops are crowned with Red Campion, knee-deep. At the doorstep of the Arctic, the Orkney Islands are a repository of both southern and northern plant-life: Bugle, Foxglove and Twayblade rub shoulders with the Oyster Plant and aromatic Scottish Lovage; on some hills of Rousay and Westray in particular may be found some unusual plant associations. *Stenness Loch* nourishes colonies of rare Spiral Tassel Pondweed.

BOWLING: Outdoor greens located at Kirkwall, Stromness and St Margaret's Hope.

BUS TOURS: A wide variety of guided tours depart from Kirkwall and Stromness, taking in many historic sites, including Maeshowe and Skara Brae, and lasting up to four hours in duration. Orkney Heritage Society periodically organise tours with an emphasis on archaeology.

CINEMA: Kirkwall has one film theatre.

CYCLING: Probably the finest way to discover Orkney: distances are moderate and terrain neither tediously hilly nor monotonously flat. Two wheels are particularly useful for getting around the outer Isles—bicyles are easily and cheaply transported by boat. Cycles may be hired in Stromness, Kirkwall and on some of the smaller Islands. Both towns are possessed of good bicycle shops, stocking spares. Cycle Touring Club hotel in Stromness.

DANCING: There is only one full-time dance hall in

TOP An inter-island flight approaching Kirkwall: *Gunnie Moberg.*
BOTTOM Another species of Orcadian aviator—Puffins: *Gunnie Moberg.*

79

Travelling in style in the early 1900s: then, as now, Orcadians were enthusiastic motorists: *Kirkwall Library*.

RECREATIONS & AMENITIES

Orkney—in Kirkwall—but both country and contemporary dances are featured in community halls and hotels every weekend. Harvest-home dances towards the end of the year are amongst the most enthusiastically supported events in the Islands, with compulsory helpings of cold meat and clapshot served out at 'half-time.' See press for details.

DIVING: Orkney provides diverse and interesting sport for the wet-suit wearer: there is much marine life, including clam and lobster, and many wrecks are dotted around its coasts—items such as old cannon are still hauled up now and again. Visibility is good, especially in winter months, and diving is possible all year round. There are many outlets for shellfish for the commercially minded. A Scottish Sub-Aqua Club branch is located at Hatston, Kirkwall, and this is equipped with two Bristol-10 compressors. Air is easily obtained from here—contact The Secretary, c/o Orkney Tourist Organisation. Workboats may be hired privately.

DRIVING: Vehicles can be transported to Orkney via the roll on/roll off Scrabster/Stromness ferry. They are also carried on the Aberdeen/Kirkwall run. Cars are freely available for hire on Mainland, besides some of the other Islands. Surfaces are good, and there is an intricate network of some 550m. of public roads. There is no shortage of garages or servicing facilities either—Orcadians are enthusiastic motorists, with one car (or tractor!) to every three head of population. Traffic lights, parking meters and traffic wardens, on the other hand, are not endemic... as yet.

EATING AND DRINKING: Orkney beef and lamb, as any chef will already know, is amongst the best in the country; seafood caught off the Islands is exported throughout Europe, America and beyond (clams, lobsters, crayfish, crabs, etc.); the home bakery is alive and well and living in Orkney—massproduced bread is, thankfully, the exception rather than the rule here; and let's not forget the ubiquitous Orcadian Oatcake or the famous farmhouse cheeses—pale, subtle and no two quite the same. All in all, some of the finest and freshest produce to be found anywhere. Although restaurants, on the whole, are not numerous, there are many hotels which cater for non-residents. Outwith the towns, and excluding hotels, sustenance can be obtained at the following places on Mainland:— *St Margaret's Hope; Tormiston* (Stenness); *Birsay; 1m. N of Tingwall* (Evie); and *2m. S of Dounby* (Harray). Fish and chip shops can be found in Kirkwall and Stromness, and a health food shop in Kirkwall caters for any remaining tastes.

The current vogue for 'real ale' has had little impact in Orkney—Orcadians have been brewing their own beer for centuries, and the distinctive redolence of the 'barley-bree' can be met with in many homes. Another local, if headier product, *Highland Park*, is a well-known single malt whisky, said to compare with brandy. (See *Industry*—distilling.) The locations of outlying licensed premises are shown on the map at the beginning of this book; Stromness has several bars to choose from, and Kirkwall many, ranging from basic, no-nonsense to brocade and reproduction brewery mirrors—a dram for all seasons...

FISHING: A sizeable percentage of Orkney's visitors are lured to the Islands by their excellent and free fishing (a legacy of ancient odal tradition and Norse law). Rivers are non-existent, but there are many fine lochs and burns, and sea-angling is unsurpassed. There are excellent tackle shops in Stromness and Kirkwall; rods can be hired here, as they may from several hotels besides. Boats are available for hire, both for sea and loch, from hotels and private owners. Orkney Trout Fishing Association offers facilities to any visiting seeker of piscatory pleasures who cares to take out temporary membership—details from The Hon. Secretary, c/o Orkney Tourist Organisation. This sporting body sponsors several evening fly-fishing contests during the season. For brown trout this extends from 15th March - 6th October; for sea trout from 26th February - 31st October. The principal lochs are Harray, Stenness, Boardhouse, Hundland, Kirbister and Swannay; smaller lochs include Isbister, Bosquoy, Sabiston, Wasdale, Clumly and Skaill (Orkney's only private loch). Usual weight of catches is around 1lb. and access to all lochs is good.

HARRAY: Most popular loch, shallow with good feeding. Mostly brown trout, some very big. Some sea trout in August and September. 14¼lb. brown trout, 14 years old, caught in 1966. Boats available from Merkister Hotel and locally. FAVOURED LOCATIONS— *Between Ling Holm and Lochside on SE bank; off Humasun Point on W bank.* FLIES—*Grouse & Claret; Blae & Black; Dunkeld; Greenwells; Black Spider; Zulu; Ke-He; Cinnamon & Gold; Invicta; Silver & Bloody Butcher; Palmer.* BEST MONTHS—*May & June.*

STENNESS: A sea-fed loch with good sea and brown trout fishing, as well as the pink-fleshed Stenness hybrid. 29¼lb. brown trout caught many years ago, plaster-cast now on display in Stromness Museum. Boats available from Standing Stones Hotel and locally. FAVOURED LOCATIONS—*Sea trout: Bridge of Waithe & Bridge of Brodgar (also salmon!); brown trout: near Ring of Brogar & Nether Bigging.* FLIES—*Ke-he; Peter Ross; Silver & Bloody Butcher; Silver Cardinal; Grouse & Claret; Dunkeld; Black Spider; Watson's Fancy; Black Pennel.* BEST MONTHS—*June & July (brown trout); July-September (sea trout).*

BOARDHOUSE: Near Birsay. Excellent brown trout fishing, with best fish caught on the water. Boats available from Barony Hotel on NE shore, and privately in Birsay. O.T.F.A. boat-hut and jetty on SW bank.

FLIES—*Dunkeld; Greenwell's Glory; Zulu; Cinammon & Gold; Black Pennel; Grouse & Claret; Butchers; Teal & Green; March Brown; Invicta; Palmer; Ke-He.* BEST MONTHS—*April-June (weed growth later).*

Of the others—SWANNAY: *Best at S. end.* HUND-LAND: *Best months May & June.* KIRKBISTER: *Good beginner's loch, esp. April-July; some salmon.* ISBISTER: *Best months May & June.* WASDALE: *ditto.* PEERIE WATER: *Best months May-July.* Apart from Mainland, the best island for loch fishing is Rousay, which is well stocked with brown trout.

SEA FISHING: There are many fish of impressive dimensions regularly landed around Orkney—e.g. halibut of 160lb. + and common skate of 200lb.+; also plaice, pollack and saithe from the shore; and ling, cod, pollack, tusk, haddock, coalfish, saithe, plaice, dogfish and mackerel from the water. Bait can be acquired from the many fish-processing plants. The main season extends from June to September, and most boats are hired from Stromness and Kirkwall. GOOD GROUNDS— *Off Copinsay, Inganess Bay, Rerwick Head, and the Northern Isles in general. Also abundant fishing to be had off the W coast of Mainland, and down the W coast of Hoy (cod, halibut and ling). In rough weather Scapa Flow is usually still fishable (skate ling and conger).* GOOD SHORE LOCATIONS—*Ayre of Quanterness (3m. NW of Kirkwall); Sebay, Tankerness (late season); Rossmyre (3m. from Kirkwall; Davie's Brig (4m. from Kirkwall); Waulkmill Bay, Orphir; Bridge of Waithe, Stenness.* Sea trout of up to 6 lb. are caught, although average weight is 1½ lb.

FOOTBALL: Contrary to common practice, this is a summer activity in Orkney; there are many local teams and fixtures, details in press. There is also an enthusiastic and well-supported rugby club in Kirkwall, with its own licensed club-house: matches are played all year round.

GOLF: Records exist of golf having taken place in Orkney as early as 1685—in the grounds of Papdale. Today, however, this sport is better catered for than then. KIRKWALL golf course—*18 holes, length 5,406 yds., par 68, open seven days a week, visitors welcome.* STROMNESS golf course—*18 holes, length 4,822 yds., par 63, open seven days a week, visitors welcome (short but challenging and very scenic).* There is also a 9 hole course on WESTRAY, near Pierowall *(closed Sundays),* and a new 9 hole course on SAN-DAY. A midnight open match is held at Kirkwall at Midsummer!

MOTORCYCLE SCRAMBLING: A local club holds fortnightly meetings on Sunday afternoons: details in the press.

MUSEUMS: Good folk museum in Kirkwall (**Tankerness House,** *open Monday-Saturday, 10.30 am - 1 pm & 2 pm - 5.30 pm, admission free*). Also an interesting little museum in Stromness, run by Orkney Natural History Society *(entrance fee);* small site museums at Skara Brae, Brough of Birsay and Gurness Broch; and a private collection of porcelain, pottery, silver, etc. at **Graemshall.**

MUSIC: Very few musical tastes are not catered for in Orkney:— St Magnus Music Festival in mid-June; Orkney Arts Society recitals and concerts; St Magnus

choral and instrumental recitals; Orkney Operatic Society; Kirkwall Pipe Band; Orkney Strathspey and Reel Society; Orkney Folk Club, et al. Also many events in hotels, etc. See press for details. Record shops in Kirkwall and Stromness.

ORNITHOLOGY: The Orkney Islands figure very large on the ornithological map of Britain: a pair of binoculars should be included in the pack list for any proposed visit here. The bird life of the secondary islands is dealt with under *The Islands,* and major bird cliffs are indicated on the map at the beginning of this book, but of Mainland the following should be said:—

The largest seabird cliffs are located at *Marwick Head* (Guillemot & Kittiwake); *Brough of Birsay; Costa Head; Black Craig; Yesnaby;* and *Mull Head,* Deerness. There are extensive mud-flats and sands at *St Peter's Pool,* Deerness much frequented by wading birds. *Loch of Harray* is one of the most important wintering grounds for Tufted Duck and Pochard in Scotland, besides Widgeon and Goldeneye. *Loch of Stenness* is also significant in this respect, and *Loch of Skaill* is one of the best for number and variety of wintering duck.

Fig. 4.—The Migratory Thrush *(Turdus migratorius).*

Over 300 species of bird have been identified in Orkney, and there are more than ninety regular breeding species. Amongst the many interesting Arctic birds which frequent the Islands are numbered Arctic and Great Skuas, Red Throated Divers and the majestic Whooper Swan, 600 or so of which arrive every October from Iceland. In addition, Hoy harbours the Manx Shearwater and the Peregrine Falcon, and Sule Skerry houses one of the largest Puffin colonies in Britain. There is a thriving Field Club in Orkney, which organises many expeditions, and interested parties should contact it, c/o Orkney Tourist Organisation.

PHOTOGRAPHY: Whether one belongs to the Box Brownie Brigade or Hasselblad Heavy Artillery, Orkney is camera country. Nevertheless, its landscape is often difficult to do justice to; photographs frequently appearing as unrelieved expanses of green and blue, neatly bisected in the horizontal plane. (N.B.—The compressing effect of a telephoto lens can work wonders here.) Neither Kodak nor the visitor need have cause for concern, however—there is an abundance of potential subject matter: picturesque nousts, quoys and winding streets; old farms and buildings; history visibly incarnate; soaring cliffs; polychrome mosaics of sea, sky and land; remarkable sunsets (esp. May-July); and faces... maps more eloquent than any folded sheet.

READING: There are public libraries in both Kirkwall and Stromness, and visitors' tickets are available. *The Orkney Room* in Kirkwall houses an extensive collection of material dealing with Orcadian, Shetland and Norse topics. There are also travelling libraries, and boxes of books are sent regularly to the outer Islands. There are several booksellers in both towns, and a bookshop in Stromness. A further reading list may be consulted at the end of this book. Orkney has had more than a generous quantity of the written word dedicated to it.

ROCK CLIMBING: Mountains in Orkney are limited to the singular—*Ward Hill* on Hoy (1,565ft.), but there are cliffs a-plenty for those intrepid enough to pack piton and karabiner. The highest sea stack in Britain—the **Old Many of Hoy** (450ft.)—was popularised by a successful, televised climb made in 1967 by Hamish McInnes, Joe Brown and others. (First conquered, however, in 1966 by Tom Patey, R. Baillie and Chris Bonington, and climbed many times since.)

SAILING: There are several enthusiastic sailing clubs in Orkney, and regular small boat regattas are staged throughout the Islands in the season. Details from Orkney Tourist Organisation. Also good chandlery stores in Kirkwall, Stromness and Longhope.

SHOPPING: The principal shopping centres are Kirkwall and Stromness. The former has branches of some larger chain stores. Other centres on Mainland and the smaller Islands have fewer stores, but such as do exist tend to stock everything from bootlaces to bicycles. Knitwear is good value, and there are many outlets. Orkney baking and confectionery is justly renowned, and homemade farmhouse cheeses are worth looking out for too. (*Early Closing:* Kirkwall - Wednesday; Stromness - Thursday.)

SQUASH: Club and courts at Hatston, Kirkwall.

SWIMMING: Indoor pools are located in Stromness and Kirkwall. Sea bathing is possible, but Orkney's waters are not always the warmest. Nevertheless, good sandy bays can be found at *Point of the Baits* (1½m. s of Kirkwall); *Waulkmill Bay,* Orphir (5m. sw of Kirkwall); *Deerness; Widewall Bay,* St Margaret's Hope; and around several of the Northern Isles (esp. *Sanday*).

TENNIS: Outdoor courts are located in Kirkwall, Stromness and St Margaret's Hope.

THEATRE: There is an Orkney Arts Theatre in Kirkwall; dramatic and operatic societies stage productions here and elsewhere. See press for details.

WALKING: Orkney caters for all breeds of perambulatory person, from the stroller of green and pleasant places to the solivagant strider. Hoy and Rousay will appeal particularly to the latter. There are many fine cliff walks too, probably the most rewarding being the coast between *Rackwick* and *St John's Head* on Hoy. Good cliff walks on Mainland include *Breckness - Broch of Borwick* (w coast, includes sea stacks •at Yesnaby and North Gaulton); vicinity of *Marwick Head* and *Birsay - Costa Head* (n coast); and *Sandside - Mull Head* (Deerness). Also Rousay (n & w coasts); Westray (w coast); and South Ronaldsay.

WATER SKI-ING: A favourite venue for this sport is sheltered *Widewall Bay,* near St Margaret's Hope.

SOME ANNUAL EVENTS

JANUARY: *Ba' Game,* Kirkwall (1st.).
JUNE: *St Magnus Festival of Music* and *Orkney Arts Festival* (mid-month).
JULY: *Stromness Shopping Week* (3rd week).
AUGUST: *Agricultural shows* (first fortnight).
AUGUST: *Boy's Ploughing Match* and *Festival of the Horse,* St Margaret's Hope (mid-month).
DECEMBER: *Ba' Game,* Kirkwall (25th.).

Services

ISOLATION! — OFF THE ORKNEYS

Southern Tourist. "Get any newspapers here?"

Orcadian Boatman. "Ou aye, when the steamer comes. If it's fine, she'll come ance a week; but when it's stormy, i' winter, we dinna catch a glint o' her for three months at a time."

S.T. "Then you'll not know what's goin' on in London!"

O.B. "Na — but ye see ye're just as ill aff i' London as we are, for ye dinna ken what's gaun on here!"

['Punch' magazine, circa 1900]

BANKS: KIRKWALL - *Clydesdale Bank, Royal Bank of Scotland, Bank of Scotland* and *Aberdeen Savings Bank.* STROMNESS - *Royal Bank of Scotland* and *Bank of Scotland.* ST MARGARET'S HOPE - *Bank of Scotland.* Also sub-offices on many islands, serviced by flying banks, and travelling banks on Mainland.

EDUCATION: In the past Orkney has produced more than its fair share of academics and eminent men and women. Learning is highly regarded in these Islands, as is the ethos of 'getting on', and a vigorous didactic tradition exists here. The reputations of Kirkwall Grammar School and Stromness Academy have carried before them, and both provide a full six-year education. There is a rather unique course in seamanship and navigation at Stromness, and a residential hostel for pupils from outlying areas located in Kirkwall. All the inhabited islands have a primary school, and part-secondary courses are taught on Hoy (North Walls), Flotta, Shapinsay, Westray, Eday, Stronsay and Sanday. There is also a special school for handicapped children at Finstown.

ELECTRICITY: Orkney is now extensively electrified since the construction of a post-war diesel power station at Kirkwall. Virtually 99 per cent of Mainland homes are connected. Other islands with mains supply are South Ronaldsay, Burray, Hoy, Rousay, Wyre, Graemsay, Sanday, Stronsay and Flotta. Electricity on the remaining inhabited islands is provided by private generators.

84

FIRE FIGHTING: Fully equipped fire stations are located in Kirkwall and Stromness. Both Mainland and the other Islands are manned by volunteer forces.

HEALTH: There are two hospitals in Orkney, both in Kirkwall. *Balfour Hospital* is general, and *Eastbank Hospital* caters for the geriatric and chronically sick. Eventide homes are located in both Stromness and Kirkwall. All the major islands have at least one doctor, and Mainland keeps eight G.P.s busy. Specialists in gynaecology, obstetrics, etc. fly in from Aberdeen to hold periodic clinics. There is an air-ambulance service to mainland Scotland, and an internal one between the islands. District nurses, health visitors and midwives tend both Mainland and the secondary Islands. Health centre and several dentists in Kirkwall.

LIBRARIES: See *Recreations & Amenities* (READING).

LIFEBOATS AND LIGHTHOUSES: Lifeboats are based at Kirkwall, Stromness and Longhope. This last-named is probably the one which, regrettably, evokes the most memories in the public imagination. On the 17th of March 1969 the Longhope lifeboat, *T.G.B.* — so named after its anonymous donor, over-turned in a force 9 gale near the Pentland Skerries whilst answering a rescue call. All eight of a crew were lost.

Stromness is the base for the Commissioners of Northern Lighthouses supply ship *Pole Star;* it services lights around Orkney, Shetland and the north of Scotland. Orkney's first lighthouse was lit in 1789 on North Ronaldsay; although disused, this still stands. Today there are twelve lighthouses around Orkney, five of which are manned, and a further nine minor lights or beacons.

NEWSPAPERS: An excellent weekly independent, *The Orcadian*, with a circulation around 10,000 copies, is published on Thursdays. Local issues are well reported and discussed; most events are advertised; and comprehensive transport timetables are printed. National newspapers are flown in every morning, except Sunday — colour supplement devotees have to wait till Monday.

POST OFFICE: Head offices are located in Kirkwall and Stromness, with many sub-offices throughout Mainland and the other Islands. First-class mail is flown in and out daily, except Sunday, and most items posted first-class usually reach their destinations in Britain the following day. Second-class mail travels by

sea. Fog, high seas, gales, etc. can occasionally hold up mail — and newspapers — for days at a time. Orkney's first post-bus operates on Rousay.

RADIO: A transmitter near Kirkwall ensures good reception throughout most of Orkney, which has its own radio broadcast on VHF (93.7 MHz) every morning, featuring local news, record requests and a 'What's On' review.

TELEVISION: 'Switched-on' Orkney now receives full colour transmissions on all channels.

TELEPHONE: The Islands are well serviced by telephone links, and altogether there are around 4,000 subscribers. All exchanges are now S.T.D. (*The Orcadian* publishes an Orkney Telephone Directory.)

TRANSPORT [EXTERNAL]: Excluding Sunday, daily flights are operated by British Airways between Orkney and Shetland, Aberdeen, Inverness, Edinburgh, Glasgow, London, Manchester *(except Saturday)* and Birmingham *(except Saturday)*. Loganair operate daily *(except Sunday)* flights to and from Wick, Inverness and Edinburgh. The main sea route is serviced by the modern roll on/roll off car ferry, *St Ola*, operated by P.& O. Ferries between Scrabster (Thurso) and Stromness. Several sailings are made daily in summer months; one in each direction in winter *(Sunday sailings during the peak season only)*. The 27m. journey lasts two hours and a very scenic course is steered past the cliffs of Hoy. The 'Ola' is named after the Norse King and Saint, Olaf, who officially converted Orkney to Christianity in 995. Services are also operated by P. &. O. from Aberdeen and Shetland to Kirkwall. A passenger ferry plies between John O'Groats and Burwick (South Ronaldsay) in summer months.

TRANSPORT [INTERNAL]: Flights are operated between Kirkwall and most of the larger Islands by Loganair *(except Sunday);* charters also available. The Orkney Islands Shipping Company is the principal inter-island sea carrier, operating boats to both the Northern and Southern Isles: there are, however, several smaller operators (for details see *The Islands* and *Useful Information*). The Southern Isles of Burray and South Ronaldsay are accessible by road, via the Churchill Barriers. Buses service most areas of Mainland, and fares are very reasonable. Cars may be hired almost anywhere, as can taxis, which are numerous, and bicycles.

Orkney Place-Names

T HE DISTINCTIVE and lilting dialect of Orkney, with its rising cadence and emphasis on the last syllable, is a legacy of the old Norse tongue—the Orkney Norn. There is no trace of Gaelic influence in it, although the discerning ear may detect an echo of the Scottish Borders. Orcadian surnames are a mixture of Norse and Scottish: such as **Firth, Flett, Foubister, Linklater, Scarth, Sclater,** and**Shea** being Norse, while **Craigie, Leask, Louttit, Pottinger** and **Spence** are Scottish. Place-names, however, are almost entirely Norse in origin. The following glossary contains some of the most common elements of these. Origins, where given, are in italics.

a & ay, see ey.
aith, isthmus.
beck, *bekkr,* stream.
bigging, *bygging,* a cluster of houses or buildings.
bister, *bólstathr,* dwelling-place, homestead.
breck, *brekka,* a slope.
brigg, *bryggja,* jetty, landing-place.
bu, an earl's or headman's homestead.
bur, edge or brim.
by or ber, *býr,* farm or estate.
clett, *klettr,* rock.
corse, a gathering fire-beacon or signal.
ey, island.
far, *faer,* sheep.
fea, see fiold.
fiold, *fjall,* hill or fell.
foul, *fugl,* bird.
garth, *garthr,* an enclosure.
geo, *gjá,* a chasm or rift.
hamar, an outcrop of rocks jutting from a hillside.
hest, *hestr,* horse or stallion.
holm, *holmr,* small island.
hope, *hóp,* bay (*lit.* 'head of a fjord').
hov, *hof,* a pagan temple.
howe, *haugr,* mound or barrow.
kame, *kamb,* a ridge.
kelda, a spring.
kir or kirk, *kirkja,* church.
knowe, tumulus or hillock.
lang, *langr,* long.
lar or ler, *leir,* clay or mud.
ling, *lyng,* heather.
lund, *lundr,* a grove.

mel, *melr,* sandbank.
muckle, large.
mull or moul, *muli,* a promontory or headland.
ness, *nes,* a headland.
nev, *nef,* nose (*lit.*), small headland (*fig.*).
noup, *gnúpr,* peak.
noust, *naust,* boat-slip or beaching-place.
os, ois, or oyce, *ós,* inlet or estuary.
papa, denotes a Celtic Christian settlement.
peerie, small.
quoy, *kvi,* outlying farm or field.
roost, *röst,* whirlpool or strong sea-current.
ros, or ross, *hross,* horse.
scarth see garth.
set or setter, *setr,* house, dwelling-place built on grazing land.
skaill, *skáli,* hall, hut or shieling.
slack, *slakki,* a shallow valley.
shun, *tjörn,* a small loch or tarn.
slat orsleat, *sletta,* plain or level field.
sten or stain, *steinn,* stone.
ston, *stadir,* steading, abode *(of).*
stor or stour, *stórr,* big.
strom, current or tide.
swart, *swartr,* dark or black.
taing, *tangi,* flat, tongue-shaped peninsula.
ting, *ping,* assembly or council.
wall or way, *vágr,* bay or creek.
ward or wart, *vartha,* site of (usu. hill) a gathering fire beacon.
wick, *vik,* bay or creek.
wra, wray or ray, *vrá,* a nook; or corner of land.

The study of Orkney farm-names and their significance is a complex subject beyond the scope of this book. The reader wishing further information would do well to obtain the works of the late Hugh Marwick: *Orkney Farm Names; The Place Names of Rousay;* and *The Place Names of Birsay.* Some idea of the chronology of farm development may be inferred from the common elements, however.

The earliest Norse settlements are indicated by a **by** suffix: **bu** and **skaill** are also primordial—the former was in most instances an earl's or headman's homestead; the latter his drinking-hall. Somewhat later on came **bister, garth, ston** and **land**: although secondary developments, these were large and important in most cases.**setter** farms represent the next stage of development and expansion, and were usually taken in from grazing land. The last category to evolve were the **quoy** farms, which were also established on former grazing land. These last frequently represent the outer limits of Norse settlement and cultivation in a locality.

Some Mainland Parishes

Birsay: 'fortress island', referring to the Brough of Birsay.

Deerness: from the bones of red deer found in peat-bogs here.

Evie: meaning 'swirl', and alluding to the fierce currents found offshore here.

Harray: deriving from 'hunting territory'.

Orphir: signifies 'place of ebbing', probably referring to the tidal island, Holm of Houton.

Rendall: meaning 'cleared valley'.

Sandwick: after the sands of Skaill Bay.

Stenness: after the standing stones at Ness of Brodgar.

Islands

Burray: 'fortress island', after the brochs here.

Copinsay: 'Kolbein's isle', after Kolbein Hruga.

Eday: 'isle of the isthmus' *(eidey)*.

Egilsay: 'holy isle', from *eaglais,* Celtic for church—or (more probable) 'Egil's isle'.

Eynhallow: 'holy island.'

Fara: 'isle of sheep'.

Flotta: 'isle of the fleet' — or 'flat island'.

Gairsay: 'Garek's isle'.

Graemsay: 'Grim's isle'.

Hoy: 'high island'.

North Ronaldsay: 'St Ringan's isle', after the Scottish saint, Ninian. Formerly known as *Rinarsey* or *Rinansey.*

Rousay: 'Hrolf's isle' or 'Rollo's isle'. Rollo became the first Duke of Normandy in 911, and was the ancestor of William the Conqueror.

Sanday: 'isle of the sands'.

Shapinsay: 'Hjalpand's isle'.

South Ronaldsay: Rognvald's isle'.

Stronsay: 'star-like island'.

Swona: 'isle of pigs'.

Wyre: 'spear-shaped island', from *vigr* or spearhead.

Orkney Recipes

CLAPSHOT

¾lb. Turnip   *1 oz. Butter*
1¼lb. Potatoes   *Salt and pepper*

PEEL AND DICE turnip. Peel potatoes. Place together in pan, cover with cold water and bring to boil. Cook for 20-30 minutes. Drain, then return to heat to steam gently. Mash together with butter, adding seasoning to taste. A little milk may be added if desired. *N.B.* Turnip will have more flavour after a frost.

ORKNEY PANCAKES

2 cups oatmeal   *2 tsp. syrup*
½ cup flour   *1 egg*
1 tsp. baking soda   *sour milk*

SOAK OATMEAL in a little sour milk for 24 hours. Add flour, soda, syrup and egg. Beat mixture, adding milk if necessary, until fairly thin. Bake on hot, greased girdle, a spoonful at a time, turning once. Delicious spread with syrup or honey. Mixture need not be used at once and will keep for some time.

BERE BANNOCKS

6 oz. beremeal   *buttermilk*
4 oz. flour   *pinch of salt*
1 tsp. baking soda

SIFT DRY ingredients together and mix with buttermilk to a soft dough. Handle gently and shape into three rounds. Place on hot, floured girdle and bake, turning once.

FLOUR BANNOCKS

10 oz. flour   *pinch of salt*
1 tsp. baking soda   *sweet milk*
1 tsp. cream of tartar   *1 tsp. melted butter*

SIFT DRY ingredients. Add melted butter and sufficient milk to make a soft dough. Handle gently and shape into three rounds. Place on hot, floured girdle and bake, turning once.

THIN OATCAKES

3 cups fine oatmeal   *dripping*
1 level tsp. baking soda   *hot water to mix*
1 level tsp. salt

MIX DRY ingredients together. To ¾ cup of this mixture add one dessert-spoon melted fat and sufficient hot water to make a soft dough. Roll out thin on an oatmeal dredged board, rubbing in plenty oatmeal. Divide into triangles with a knife and bake on a hot girdle, finishing off in front of a fire or under a low grill: or bake in a moderate oven for 20-30 minutes, turning once.

It's best to mix a little at a time in this way, as dough hardens quickly. As one batch is being baked another may be prepared. If desired, bannocks may be made instead, simply by rolling mixture out less thinly, i.e. ¼in.-½in. thick. Bake in same manner.

(Recipes by Mrs. Irene Sinclair)

Further Reading

GENERAL

Orkney Hugh Marwick ROBERT HALE 1951
Orkney & Shetland Eric Linklater ROBERT HALE 1965
The New Orkney Book ed. John Shearer NELSON & SONS 1966
Orkney Patrick Bailey DAVID & CHARLES 1971
Orkney Ronald Millar BATSFORD 1976
The Northern Isles: Orkney and Shetland Alexander Fenton JOHN DONALD 1978

HISTORY & ARCHAEOLOGY

The Ancient Monuments of Orkney Anna & Graham Ritchie HMSO 1978
Orkney & Shetland — An Archaeological Guide Lloyd Laing DAVID & CHARLES 1974
Guide to Prehistoric Scotland Richard Feachem BATSFORD 1977
The Northern Isles F.T. Wainwright 1962
The Folklore of Orkney & Shetland Ernest W. Marwick BATSFORD 1975
History of the Orkney Islands (first published 1805) George Barry MERCAT PRESS 1974
The Orkneyinga Saga (a) translated by Hjaltalan & Goudie MERCAT PRESS 1977 (b) translated by
    Palsson & Edwards HOGARTH PRESS 1978

NATURAL HISTORY

The Natural Environment of Orkney NATURE CONSERVANCY COUNCIL 1975
Orkney & Shetland—British Regional Geology HMSO 1976
Orkney Birds—Status & Guide E. Balfour CHARLES SENIOR 1972
Birds & Mammals of Orkney William Groundwater KIRKWALL PRESS 1974
Orkney Shore Robert Rendall KIRKWALL PRESS repub. 1973

MISCELLANEOUS

Reminiscences of an Orkney Parish (first published 1920) John Firth ORKNEY NAT· HIST· SOC· 1972
Stromness — Late 19th Century Photographs ORKNEY NAT· HIST· SOC· 1972
The Place Names of Birsay Hugh Marwick ABERDEEN UNIV· PRESS 1970
Eynhallow—The Holy Island of the Orkneys John Mooney KIRKWALL PRESS repub. 1976
Island Saga—The Story of North Ronaldsay Mary A. Scott A·P· REID & SON 1968
The Collected Orkney Dialect Tales of C.M. Costie KIRKWALL PRESS 1976
The Boy with the Bronze Axe Kathleen Fidler PUFFIN 1968
The Hogboon of Hell and other strange Orcadian Tales Nancy & W. Towrie Cutt ANDRE DEUTSCH 1979

GEORGE MACKAY BROWN

An Orkney Tapestry VICTOR GOLLANCZ/QUARTET 1969
Letters from Hamnavoe GORDON WRIGHT 1975
Under Brinkie's Brae GORDON WRIGHT 1979
Portrait of Orkney CHATTO & WINDUS (forthcoming)
NOVELS & SHORT STORIES: *A Calendar of Love* (1967) *A Time to Keep* (1969) *Greenvoe*
    (1972) *Magnus* (1973) *Hawkfall* (1974) *The Two Fiddlers* (1974) *The Sun's Net* (1976)
    Pictures in the Cave (1977) CHATTO & WINDUS
POEMS: *Fishermen with Ploughs* (1971) *Winterfold* (1976) *Selected Poems* (1977) CHATTO &
    WINDUS

Useful Information

TRANSPORT

British Airways: *reservations* - 69 Albert Street, Kirkwall. Tel. 3359. *Flight enquiries* - Kirkwall Airport. Tel. 2233.

Loganair: *reservations and enquiries* - Kirkwall Airport. Tel. 3025. *charters* - Tel. 2420. Telex 75121.

P & O Ferries: Pierhead, Stromness. Tel. 850655. Telex 75221. *also* Harbour Street, Kirkwall. Tel. 3330. Telex 75296.

Orkney Islands Shipping Co.: 4 Ayre Road, Kirkwall. Tel. 2044. Telex 75193. *also* - 22 John Street, Stromness. Tel. 850381.

John O'Groats/S. Ronaldsay ferry: Thomas & Bews, Ferry Office, John O'Groats. Tel. J. O'G. 353 (summer) & Barrock 619 (winter).

Stromness/Hoy ferry: Mr Moat, 126 Victoria Street, Stromness. Tel. 850678, 850276 or 850624.

Tingwall/Rousay/Egilsay/Wyre ferry: Mr Magnus Flaws, Helziegetha, Wyre. Tel. Rousay 203.

Kirkwall/Shapinsay ferry: Tel. Balfour 230.

ORGANISATIONS

Tourist Information Offices: (I) Broad Street, Kirkwall. Tel. 2856. (II) Pierhead, Stromness. Tel. 850716. (III) St Margaret's Hope. Tel. 351.

Kirkwall Health Centre: Balfour Hospital, Kirkwall. Tel. 2763.

Consumer Protection Department: Old Scapa Road, Kirkwall. Tel. 2843.

Orkney Council of Social Services: 11 Broad Street, Kirkwall. Tel. 2897.

Legal Aid: 5 Broad Street, Kirkwall. Tel. 3151.

Danish & German Consul: J.D.M. Robertson, Shore Street, Kirkwall. Tel. 2961.

Norwegian & Netherlands Consul: W.J. Jolly, 21 Bridge Street, Kirkwall. Tel. 2268.

Police: in emergency dial 999, otherwise Tel. Kirkwall 2241, Stromness 850222 or Longhope 222.

'The Orcadian' (newspaper): Victoria Street, Kirkwall. Tel. 3249.

Occidental of Britain Inc.: 3 Castle Street, Kirkwall (P.O. Box 14). Tel. 3518. Flotta terminal - Tel. Longhope 341. Telex 75212.

HOSTELS

S.Y.H.A.
KIRKWALL: Old Scapa Road - *open May/September - 100 beds - grade 2.*
STROMNESS: Town Hall - *open May/September - 54 beds - grade 2.*

Youth & Community Service: Education Offices, Albert Street, Kirkwall. Tel. 3141.
BIRSAY: *organised groups only - open March/September - 24 beds - grade 3.*
HOY (LINKSNESS): *open mid-March/mid-September - 20 beds - grade 3.*
HOY (RACKWICK): *open mid-March/mid-September - 8 beds - grade 3.*

Private
STROMNESS: *open all year - 16 beds.* (Mrs Brown, 30 Victoria Street, Tel. 850475.)
SANDWICK: *open all year - 28 beds.* (Mrs Garson, Quoyloo. Tel. 614.)

USEFUL INFORMATION

EVIE: *open all year - 20 beds.* (Mrs Taylor, Flaws. Tel. 208.)

SOUTH RONALDSAY (HERSTON): *open all year - 12 beds.* (Hiker's Hostel, Herston. Tel. St. Margaret's Hope 208.)

ROUSAY: *open all year - 6 beds.* (Mrs Swann, Broland Hostel, Cruannie. Tel. Rousay 304.)

EDAY: *open April/September - 12 beds.* (Mrs Gray, School Place. Tel. Eday 223 or 227.)

WYRE: *open June/September - 8 beds.* (Mrs Flaws, Caravelle. Tel. Rousay 203.)

CAMP & CARAVAN SITES

KIRKWALL: ½m. w of town of Grainbank *(facilities).*

STROMNESS: 1m. s of town-centre at Point of Ness *(facilities).*

ROUSAY: NE side of island at Sourin *(camp site only - facilities - tent, car & bicycle hire - no dogs).*

ALSO

Weather Reports: Kirkwall Airport. Tel. Kirkwall 2421, ext. 34 or 35.

Kirkwall & Stromness S.T.D. Code: 0856 *(external).*

Scotland's airline

GLASGOW -	BARRA	ISLAY
	SKYE	TIREE
	CAMPBELTOWN	
INVERNESS -	EDINBURGH	
	WICK	KIRKWALL
WESTERN ISLES -	STORNOWAY	
	BENBECULA BARRA	
SHETLAND -	INTER ISLAND	
ORKNEY -	INTER ISLAND	
ABERDEEN -	OIL SERVICES	

350 flights a week to 27 destinations

LOGANAIR

Ask your travel agent
for details or telephone
041 889 3181 for timetable

VISIT ORKNEY'S MOST INTRIGUING GIFT CENTRE

and choose from our wide range of
CRAFT-MADE GOODS
including beautifully fashioned and finished
ORKNEY JEWELLERY
in silver & gold,
LOCAL POTTERY
—unusual designs with practical uses,
and many other craft-made items at prices to suit all pockets.

41/43 VICTORIA STREET, STROMNESS
TEL. STROMNESS (0856) 850391

Also:
Real & Costume Jewellery—Watches & Clocks
Silver Plate—Cut Glass
Household Ware—Fancy Goods
Shopping Bags & Handbags—Toys (educational & entertaining)
Records—Cassettes—Film
&c., &c.

If it wasn't for the Clydesdale Bank ...

... thousands of personal current account customers would be paying service charges.

Why not call in at your local Ciydesdale Bank and find out for yourself?

Clydesdale Bank

Kirkwall Branch:
3 Broad Street. D. S. Gauld, Manager.
The bank that's nearest to you and your needs.

94

The ARTIST'S STUDIO

ST. MARGARET'S HOPE

★ ★ ★

PAINTINGS OF ORKNEY
by JOHN CARTMEL-CROSSLEY

★ ★ ★

Watercolours—Oils—Etchings—Prints
Enamelling—Photography*—Artist's Materials
Pottery—Ceramics
Books on Artists' Techniques
&c., &c.

★ ★ ★

Commissions accepted for paintings of local
landscapes, portraiture, design-work &c.

★ ★ ★

Individual tuition & tuition by post.

★ ★ ★

Details from: **The Artist's Studio, Front Road**
Tel. St. Margaret's Hope 381
*Commercial & Portrait

Royal Hotel

VICTORIA STREET, KIRKWALL

CENTRALLY SITUATED

H & C IN ALL ROOMS

FULL LICENSED

OPEN ALL YEAR

TELEPHONE:
KIRKWALL 3477 (0856) — OFFICE
KIRKWALL 2377 (0856) — VISITORS

Taversoe Hotel
Rousay
B & B and FULL BOARD
BAR MEALS—SANDWICHES—COFFEE
FULLY LICENSED
Peaceful Location near Historic Sites
Splendid Panoramic View of Mainland
Telephone: ROUSAY 325

❧ KELDROSEED ❧

SANDWICK, STROMNESS   Telephone: SANDWICK 628

Not an hotel, but a comfortable family house where discerning guests who enjoy good food are welcome.

Beautifully situated on the shores of the Loch of Stenness, Keldroseed is ideal for trout fishing, bird watchint, cliff and country walks, archaeology, or just doing nothing. There are residential courses in spinning and weaving, fly fishing and fly tying.

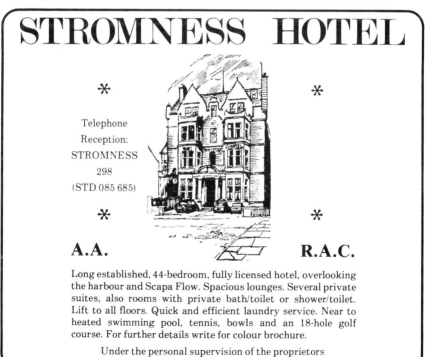

You can always be sure of a warm welcome
at

The POMONA INN
Finstown

FULLY LICENSED

from
Maurice & Jean

*TELEPHONE
FINSTOWN 201*

The Old Ship Inn

SALAD AND COFFEE HOUSE
LICENSED RESTAURANT

★ ★ ★

7 BRIDGE STREET, KIRKWALL
Telephone Kirkwall 3184

BAR
RESTAURANT
ACCOMMODATION
EFFICIENT
SERVICE

HOSPITALITY
OVERLOOKING
TOWN
EXCELLENT
LOCATION

Ideal centre for touring Orkney. Open all year.
H & C in all bedrooms. Central-heating throughout.
Convenient for golf-course. Trout-fishing & sea-angling arranged.
Non-residents welcome.
PROPRIETORS: MR & MRS D. TAIT
BRAES HOTEL, STROMNESS, ORKNEY. TEL: STROMNESS 850495

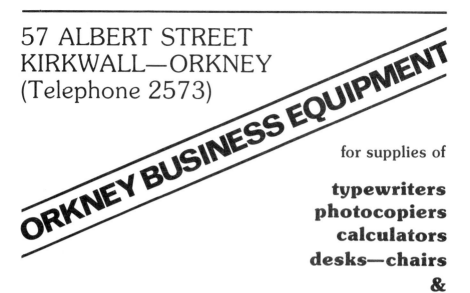

All part of the service

Managing your money. A Current (or Cheque) Account is the first step.
Your salary or wages can be paid in direct. And you can keep a tight check on your spending.
It's an easy, convenient and up-to-date way to look after your money.

No need to be unsure about insurance.
Our Managers, backed by a team of
insurance consultants, can help make sure
with insurance cover to suit your needs
and budget.

SCOTBUDGET COVERS BILLS SUCH AS THESE:
Electricity
Heating
Rates
Telephone
School Fees
Life Assurance
Car / House Insurance
Season Tickets
Motor Tax Licence
TV Rental and Licence
Annual Subscriptions (Golf etc.)
Freezer Supplies
You may also budget for:
Holidays
Christmas Expenses
Clothing
Car Servicing / Repairs

Meeting those bills. Scotbudget is the answer.
A special service to help you pay all those bills as
and when they become due. It's a big worry-saver!

Saving with interest. Regular transfers of
funds from your Current Account into a Deposit
Account will help your money grow. And you can
withdraw all or part whenever you need it.

Holiday or business travel.
Taking travellers cheques is better than taking chances. We can arrange your
travel insurance cover too. Ask us about Scot-travel before you go.

These are just a few of the services you can get with Bank of Scotland.

We call them Scotservices.

There are many more, and they are all designed to help make your life a little easier.

Call at your nearest Bank of Scotland branch and find out how Scotservices can really work for you.

The Manager and his staff will be pleased to help and advise you.

It's all part of our service.

BANK OF SCOTLAND

100

102

BABY LINEN
52 Dundas Street, Stromness. Tel. 850255
BABY SPECIALISTS
CHILDREN'S FASHIONS — Tots to Teens
LADIES — Knitwear, Blouses & Underfashions

JAMES M. CROY
43 & 46 Victoria Street, Kirkwall. Tel. 2925
CARPETS
FURNITURE
HOUSEHOLD DRAPERY

D. WISHART & SON
The Garage, Stromness. Tel 850224
AUSTIN/MORRIS DEALERS — RALEIGH CYCLES
SELF-DRIVE HIRE CARS
BOOKING AGENTS, BRITISH AIRWAYS

ORKNEY TELEVISION ENTERPRISE
17 Broad Street, Kirkwall. Tel 2613
& 113 Victoria Street, Stromness. Tel. 850555
RECORDS & TAPES
HI-FI & COLOUR TV

JOHN KEMP (DRAPERS)
28 Albert Street, Kirkwall. Tel. 3190
TRADITIONAL HANDKNITTED LACE SCARFS
FAIR ISLE GLOVES & MITTS
ORKNEY DISHTOWELS

ORKNEY FIELD & ARTS CENTRE, BIRSAY.
Tel. Birsay 221
ACCOMMODATES INDIVIDUALS AS WELL AS GROUPS

THE PALACE TEAROOMS, BIRSAY.
Tel. Birsay 221
OPEN FROM 11 am DAILY
LUNCHES AND TEAS — HOME COOKING
BED AND BREAKFAST

Ortak

—Scotland's leading manufacturers of Silver, Gold and Stone Jewellery.

Hatston Industrial Estate
Kirkwall—Orkney
Telephone Kirkwall 2224 (0856)

Our factory is open to visitors:
Monday to Friday: 9.30 am - 12.30 pm & 2 pm - 4.30 pm.
We shall be pleased to have you visit us during your stay.

The Ortak Giftshop adjoins the Factory:
Open Monday to Friday: 9 am - 1 pm & 2 pm - 5 pm.
Saturdays: 10 am - 1 pm & 2 pm - 5 pm.

Full range of ORTAK Silver, Gold and Stone Jewellery and other gifts for all occasions.
Trade Brochure Available.

BOOKS TO HELP YOU ENJOY YOUR HOLIDAY

HIGHLAND LANDFORMS
Robert J. Price

1976, £2.79
112 pp, 48 colour and 31 black & white photographs,
10 maps and five diagrams.

  Geographer and landforms expert Robert Price communicates his fascination with the shape and shaping of one of the most freshly-minted landscapes in Europe. He deals with the Highlands and Islands on an area-by-area basis.

HIGHLAND FLORA
Derek Ratcliffe

1977, £3.80
112 pp, 48 colour and 30 black & white photographs and a map.

HIGHLAND BIRDS
Desmond Nethersole-Thompson

3rd edition, 1978, £3.80
112 pp, 62 colour and 20 black and white photographs, maps, index.

EXPLORE THE HIGHLANDS AND ISLANDS

1977, £1.30
64pp, 95 colour and 19 black & white photographs, 11 maps.

Published by the Highlands and Islands Development Board, Bridge House, Bank Street, Inverness and available direct or in book and gift shops.

Where to stay on your way over to Orkney.

To: P&O Ferries, Box 2, Feltham, Middlesex, TW14 0TG.
I'd like to know more about the comfortable lounge, bar and cafeteria that make St. Ola the best place to stay between Scrabster and Stromness.

As you're the only company that operates a car ferry to Orkney, I'd also like to know more about your regular, frequent sailings throughout the week. So please send me one of your free colour brochures.

Name_____

Address_____

_____

OOB 1

P&O Ferries
TO ORKNEY

A great deal from a great company.

STROMNESS B∞KS & PRINTS

1 GRAHAM PLACE,

STROMNESS

TEL: 850565

We stock an extensive range of hardbacks and paperbacks
to suit all tastes, interests and ages
+ *books on Orkney, maps, cards, etc.*

ADVERTISING INDEX